# Osamu Iwaya's Calligraphy

## SENJIMON IN 3 STYLES

TRANSLATED BY

*Hideo Muranaka*

authorHOUSE

AuthorHouse™
1663 Liberty Drive
Bloomington, IN 47403
www.authorhouse.com
Phone: 1 (800) 839-8640

© 2019 Hideo Muranaka. All rights reserved.

No part of this book may be reproduced, stored in a retrieval system, or transmitted by any means without the written permission of the author.

Published by AuthorHouse  10/22/2019

ISBN: 978-1-7283-3290-1 (sc)
ISBN: 978-1-7283-3289-5 (hc)
ISBN: 978-1-7283-3291-8 (e)

Library of Congress Control Number: 2019917284

Print information available on the last page.

Any people depicted in stock imagery provided by Getty Images are models, and such images are being used for illustrative purposes only.
Certain stock imagery © Getty Images.

This book is printed on acid-free paper.

Because of the dynamic nature of the Internet, any web addresses or links contained in this book may have changed since publication and may no longer be valid. The views expressed in this work are solely those of the author and do not necessarily reflect the views of the publisher, and the publisher hereby disclaims any responsibility for them.

# Osamu Iwaya's Calligraphy Senjimon in 3 Styles
## Translated by Hideo Muranaka

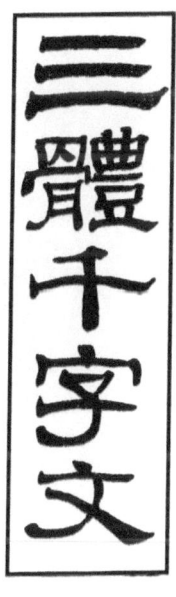

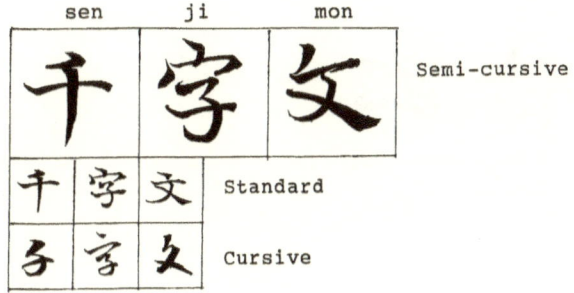

One thousand character poems.
sen(千 qiān)thousand,a great number.
ji(字 zi)character,word,name,form of written
mon,bun(文 wen)script,character,writing,language,
literary composition,literary language,culture.
This book was edited by Shu Ko Shi( 周興嗣 zhōu xing si) who
was collected poems.

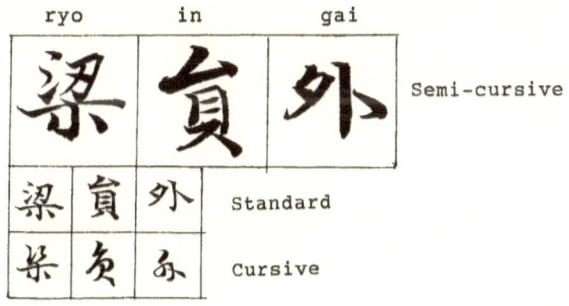

ryo(梁 liáng)beam,ridge,ray,balance beam.
in(員 yuán)a person engaged in some field activity,member,
related to a circle,in charge,surroundings.
gai(外 wai)outside,other,foreign,external,far,relatives of
one's mother,unofficial,besides,in addition,beyond.

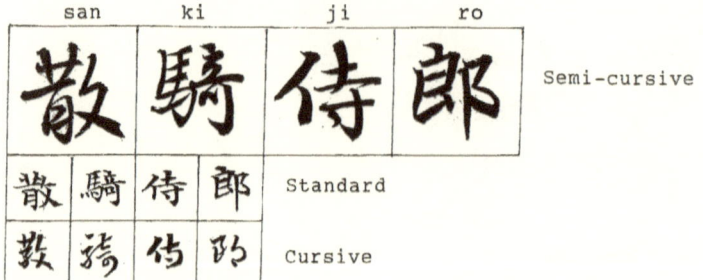

He was given a specified position like horse-riding watching people.  san(散 sàn)give,come loose,scattered,dark,undisciplined, break,useless, sanpei(散兵 san bing)skirmisher. ki(騎 qi)ride on( animal or bicycle),(ji)be on horseback,ride on a horse. ji(侍 shi)wait,attend upon,serve,warrior, ro(郎 làng)an ancient official title,referring to certain kinds of people,pet address by woman to her husband or lover(my daring)the name of place during Shunshu(春秋 chun qiu)the Spring and Autumn Period 770 B.C. - 476 B.C.

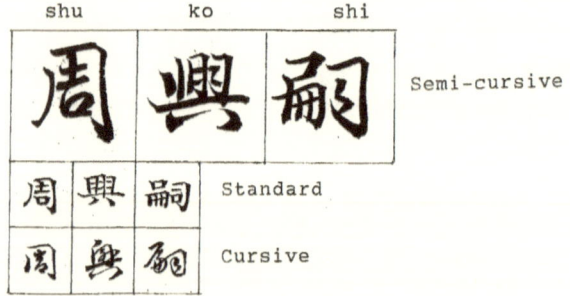

Shukoshi(周興嗣 zhōu xing si), he was born during the Ryo(梁 liang 502 - 557) Dynasty and got specified position except the fixed positions. First his role was horse-riding watching ordinary people, afterward he acquired the position of chamberlain in life. Under Butei( 武帝wu di 464 - 549 ), his pen name was Sisan(思纂 sī zuǎn).  shu(周 zhōu)all over,circumference,all around,save, truth,reach,be thorough, ko(興 xing)prosper,get up,begin,promote, become popular,interesting,be glad at, shi(嗣 si)suceed,heir, inherit,descendant.

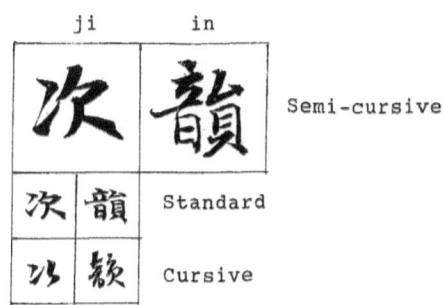

ji( 次 cì )order,sequence,second,next,number of times,frequency, lodge,dwelling,inn,stars,between, in( 韻 yun )rhyming,charm,metre in verse,rules of rhyming,taste, jiin( 次韻 ) means someone's poems or to compose poems by using another person's poems or rhyming.

Five Butei( 武帝 wu di) emperors are known.
1. Butei:   Kobutei( 孝武帝 xiào wu di) 140 B.C. - ?
            Kanbutei( 漢武帝 hán wu di)
2. Butei:   Soso( 曹操 cao cao) 154 - 220 = Motoku( 孟德 mèng dé)
3. Butei:   Shibaen( 司馬炎 si mǎ yuan) 236 - 290
4. Butei:   Ryuyu( 劉裕 liú yù) 356 - 422
5. Butei:   Shoen( 蕭衍 xiao yǎn) 464 - 549

1.

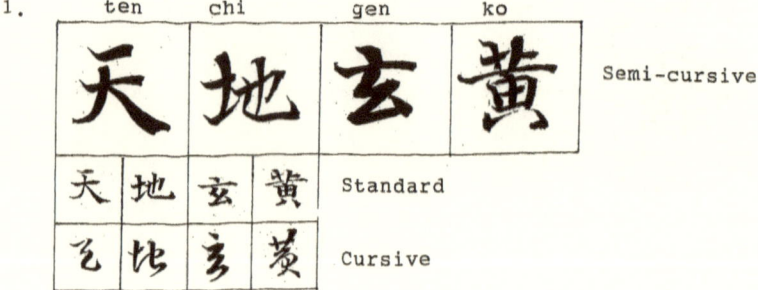

Heaven and earth are black and yellow.
ten(天 tiān)sky,heaven,day,god, chi(地 di)the earth,land,soil,
field,position, gen(玄 xuan)profound,black,skillful, ko(黄 huáng)
yellow,gold,decadent,cereals,Yellow Emperor.

2.

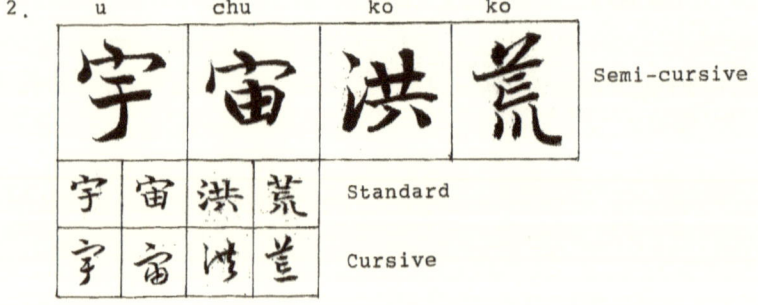

The Universe is vast and boundless.
u(宇 yǔ)housing,space,glob,sky,big, chu(宙 zhòu)sky,heaven,space,
time, ko(洪 hóng)big,vast,flood,high,very, ko(荒 huāng)wide,
uncultivated,wasteland,famine,rough.

3.

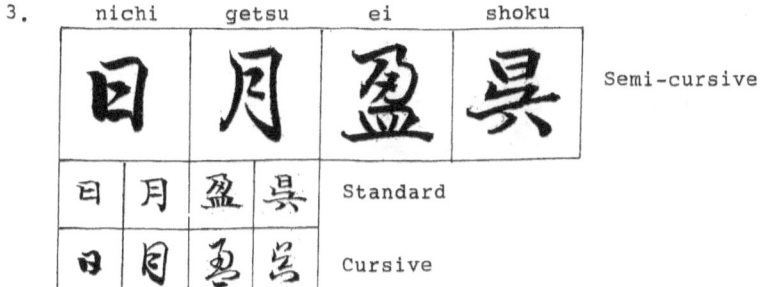

The sun declines westward and the moon is full.
nichi(日 ri)the sun,sunlight,a day,days,Japan, getsu(月 yùe)the moon,
month,moonlight,,time, ei(盈 yíng)flow,fill,overflow,remains, shoku(昃
zè)decline,afternoon.lean.

4.

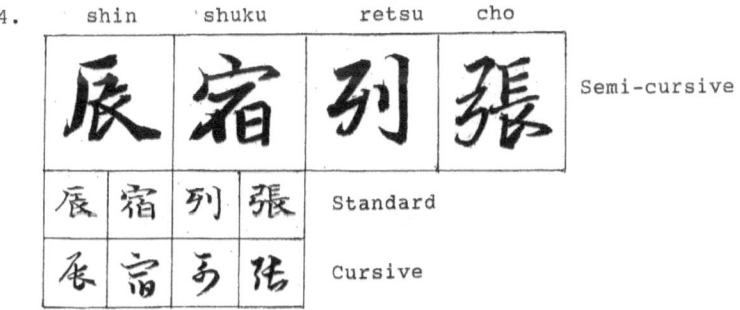

The stars are suspended in the sky.
The stars mean Hokkyokusei(北極星 bei jí xing) the North Star(the
Pole Star).  shin(辰 chén)dragon,March,8a.m.,8a.m - 10a.m.,time,
early morning, shuku(宿 sù)conceive,stars,stay in,old,in advance,
retsu(列 liè)distribute,range,arrange, cho(張 zhàng)curtain,
shop-curtain,drawing-curtain,notebook.

5.

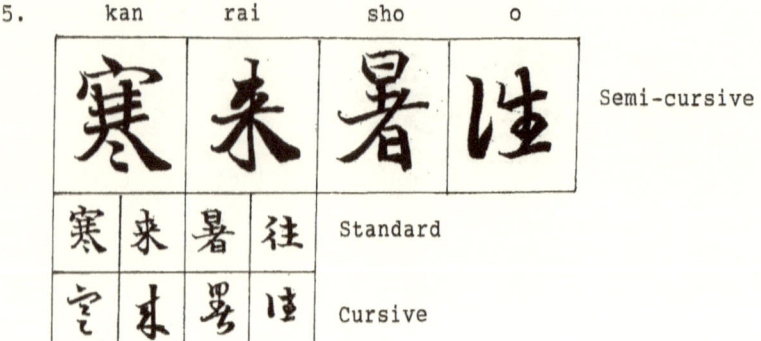

The heat(summer) left and the cold(winter) has come.
kan(寒 hán)old,afraid,poor, rai(来 lái)come,arrive, sho(暑 shǔ)
heat,weather, ou(往 wǎng)go,direction.

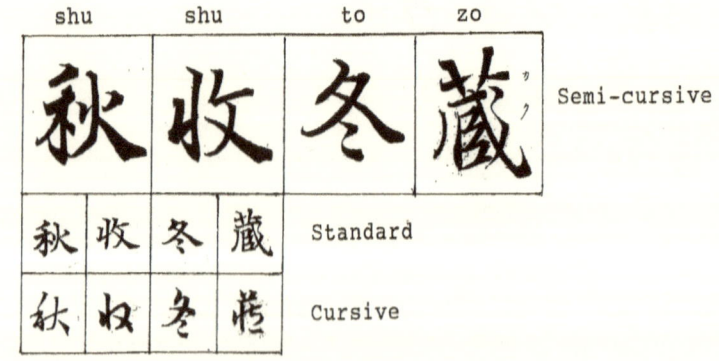

In autumn we reap a harvest and have it in store for the winter.
shu(秋 qiu)autumn,harvest time, shu(收 shōu)receive,collect,
harvest, to(冬 dōng)winter,winter sleep, zo(藏 cáng)hide,store,
a collection.

7.    jun      yo      sei      sai

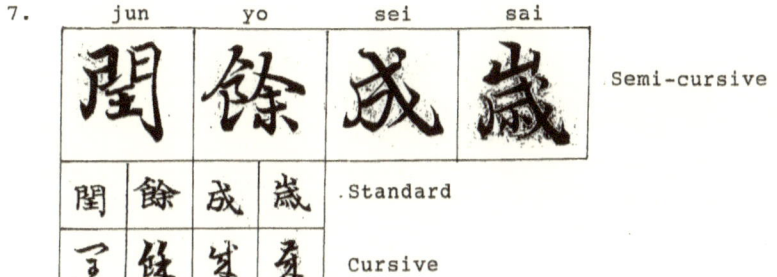

Semi-cursive

Standard

Cursive

We decide the year of a leap month(every 3 years in the lunar
calendar).   jun(閏 rùn)astron,leap, junnen(閏年 rùn nian)leap
year, junjitsu(閏日 rùn ri)leap day, jungetsu(閏月 rùn yue)
intercalary month in the lunar calendar, yo(餘 yú)I,me,a surname,
remaining,more than,over, sei(成 chéng)accomplish,succeed,establish,
ready-made,all right, sai(歲 sùi)year,year of age,the year's harvest.


8.    ritsu     ro      cho      yo

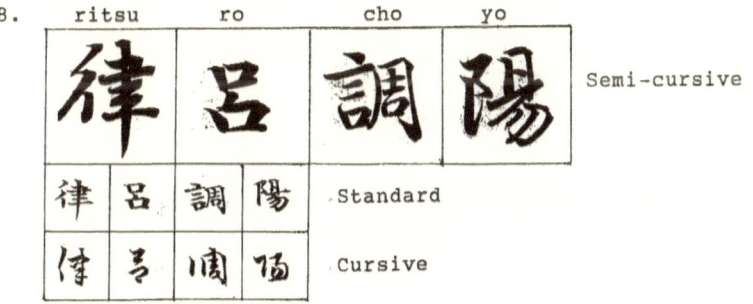

Semi-cursive

Standard

Cursive

High-pitched sounds(yo 陽 yang: 6) and low-pitched sounds(in 陰 yin:
6 ) harmonize with the balance of sunlight and shade. The sounds
mean 12 months.   ritsu(律 lu)law,rule,pitched-pipe used in ancient
music, ryo,ro(呂 lǔ)a surname,(ritsuro 律呂 lulu)a series of 12
bamboo pitch-pipes used in ancient music, cho(調 diao)transfer,
move,accent,(music: the key of C),air,melody, yo(陽 yang)yang,
the masculine,positive principle in nature,(opp in 陰       yin)
the sun,south of a hill, koyo(衡陽 heng yang: a city situated
on the south side of kozan(恒山 heng shan) in Sanseisho(山西省
shan xi sheng) Shanxi Province.

9.

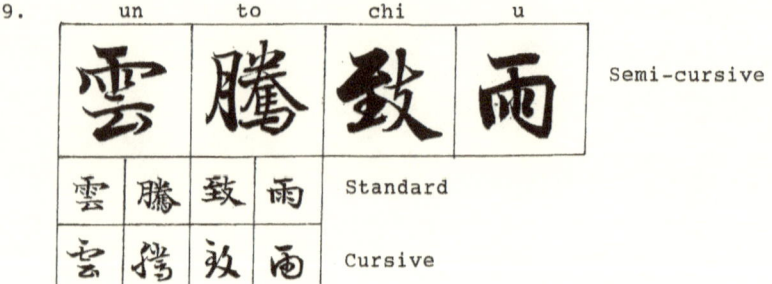

The clouds rise and become the rain.
un(雲 yún)cloud, to(騰 téng)gallop,jump,rise,make room,chi(致 zhì)send,deliver,incur, u(雨 yǔ)rain,snow.

10.

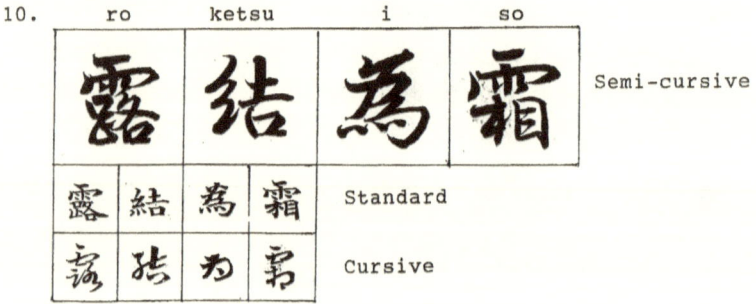

The dew congeals and forms the frost.
ro(露 lù)dew,fruit or leaves,show,betray, ketsu(結 jié)tie,knot, congeal,settle,electron, i(爲 wéi)do,act,become,part, so(霜 shuāng)frost,frostlike,white.

11.

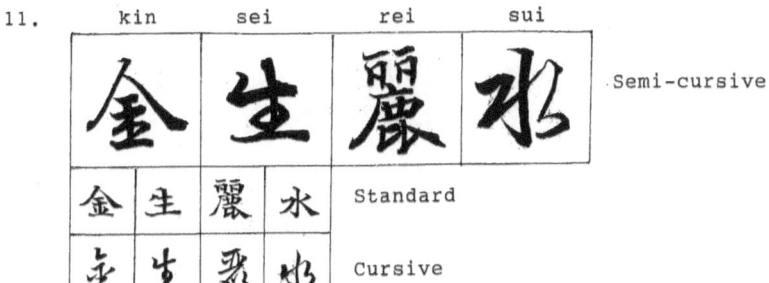

The gold is found in Reisui River.
kin(金 jīn)metal,money,gold,highly respected,the Jin Dynasty
1115 - 1234, sei(生 shēng)beat,be born,grow,alive,, rei(麗 lì)
beautiful,depend on, sui(水 shuǐ)water,river,lakes,a surname.


12.

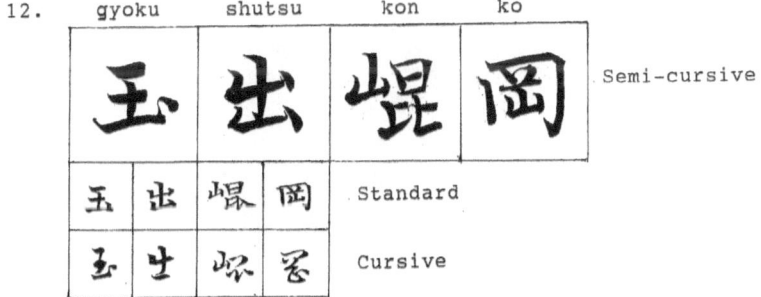

Gem stones are found in Mt.Konron(崑崙 kūn lun shān).
gyoku(玉 yù)jade,honor,handsome,beautiful, shutsu(出 chu)produce,
ko(崗 gang)slope,a hill. konko(崑崗 kūn gang = Mt.Konron(kūn lun shān).

13.

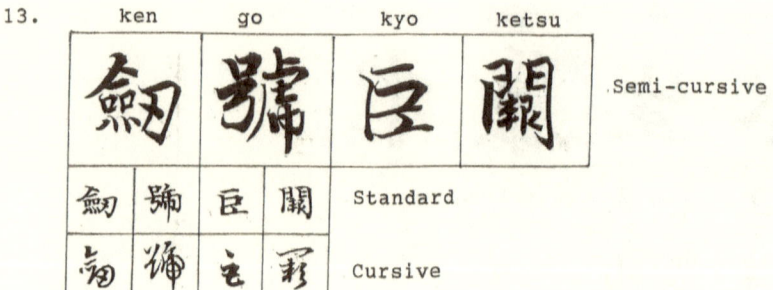

We call the sword " Kyoketsu ".
ken(劍 jìan)sword,sabre, go(號 hào)name,business,mark,sign,size,
business house,personal, kyo(巨 jù)huge,tremendous, ketsu(闕
què)imperial palace,watchtower on either side of a palace gate.

14.

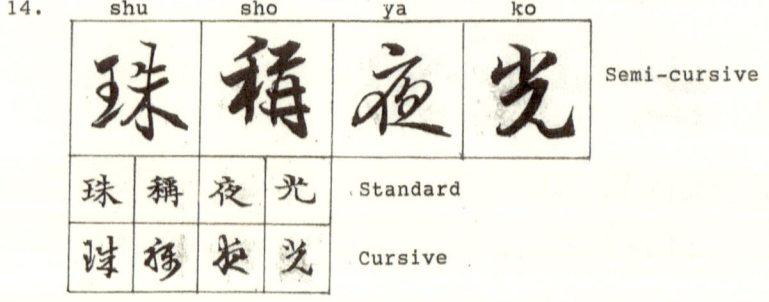

Gem stones are named " Yako 夜光 the light of night ".
shu(珠 zhū)pearl,bead, sho(稱 cheng)fit,estimate,balance,name,
ya(夜 yè)night,evening, ko(光 guāng)light,glory,brightness,bare.

15.

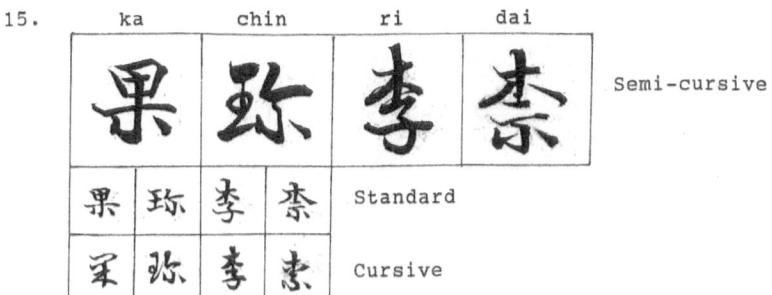

8.a
We think that damson(plum) and apple are rare among the fruit.
ka(菓 guǒ)fruit,result,resolute,indeed,as expected, chin(珍 zhen)treasure,valuable,rare, ri(李 lǐ)plum,a surname, dai(柰 nai)a kind of apple.

16.

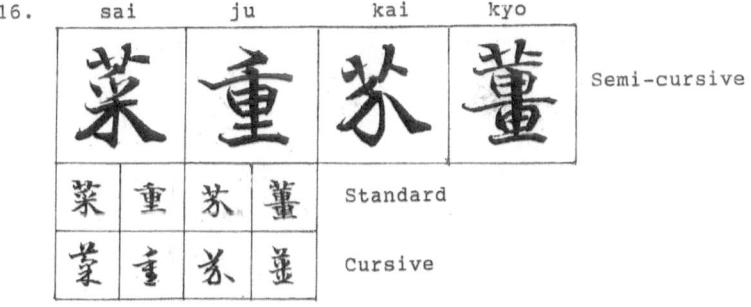

Mustard and ginger are very important among vegetables.
sai(菜 cài)vegetables,wild herbs,vegetable dish, ju(重 zhòng) weight,heavy,important,deep,discreet, kai(芥 jiè)mustard, kyo(薑 jiang)ginger.

17.

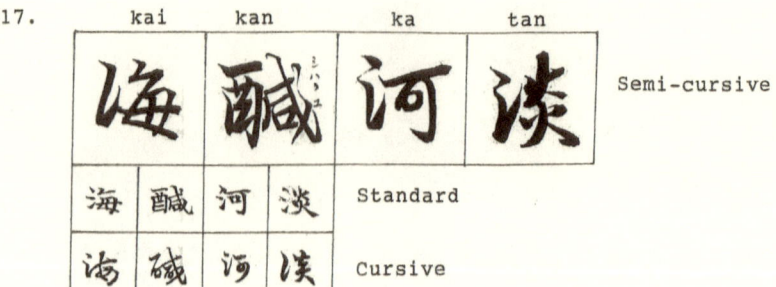

Sea water is salty and fresh water is mild.
kai(海 hǎi)sea,big lake, kan(醶 xián)salty, ka(河 hé)river,
the Milky Way System,the Yellow River, tan(淡 dàn)thin,light,
tasteless,weak,pale,meaningless.

18.

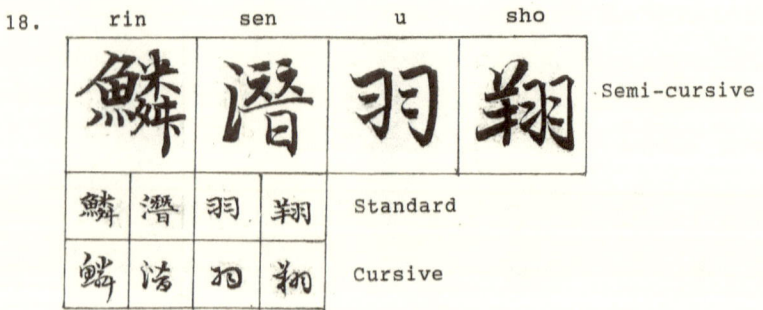

Fish hide themselves in the water and birds fly in the sky.
rin(鱗 lín)fish,scales, sen(潛 qián)hide,hidden,secretly, u(羽
yǔ)bird,feather,plum,help,shuttlecock, sho(翔 xiáng)circle in
the air,hover.

19.

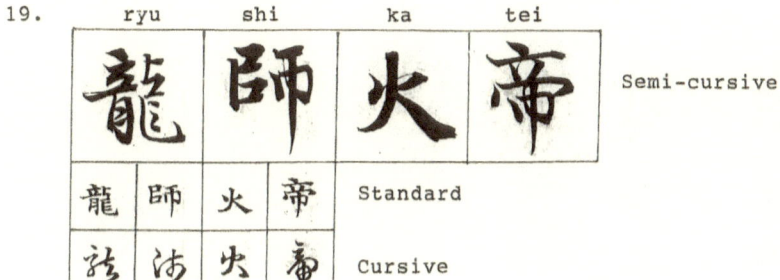

Ryushi(the position of dragon) and Katei(the father of cooking). Here ka(火 fire) came to mean Kashoku(火食: to cook by using fire), because Suijin(燧人 sui ren)'s nickname is the emperor of fire 火帝. ryu(龍 long)dragon,imperial, shi(師 shi)teacher, position,master,troops, ka(火 huǒ)fire,temper, tei(帝 di)emperor, god.

20.

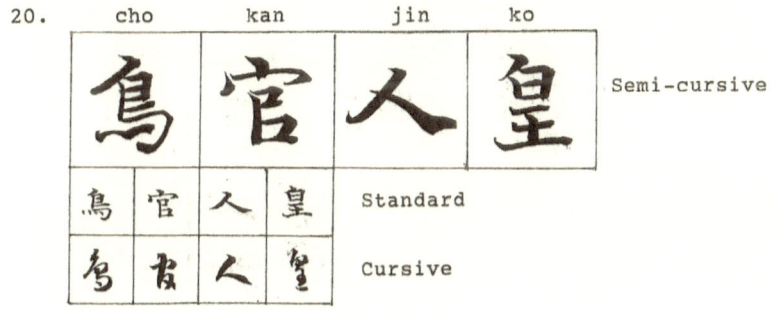

Phoenix is the symbol of good fortune.
chokan(the position of bird:phoenix) and jinko(Emperor and his deputies:Sanko 三皇 sūn huang). Sanko 1.tenno(天皇 tīan huáng) 2.jiko(地皇 di huang) 3.jinko(人皇 ren huáng) or a.Fukugi(伏羲 fuxi) b.Shinno(神農 shen nong) c.Kotei(黄帝 huang di). Shinno = Entei(炎帝 yán di).

21.   shi   sei   mo   ji

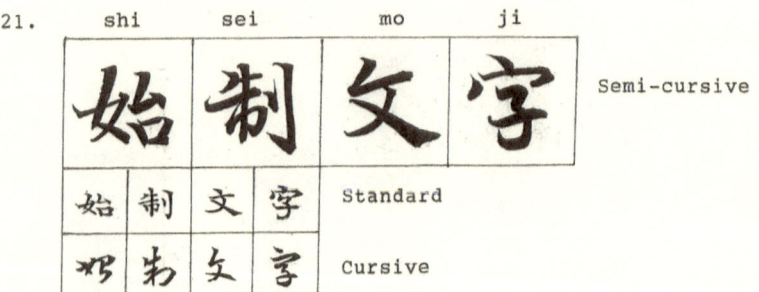

Semi-cursive
Standard
Cursive

chuang
We established characters for the first time. Soketsu(創頡 xie) invented characters after he saw bird's footprint as a legend.
shi(始 shǐ)begin, sei(制 zhì)work out,formulate,make, mon(文 wén) character,language, ji(字 zì)word,character.


22.   dai   fuku   i   sho

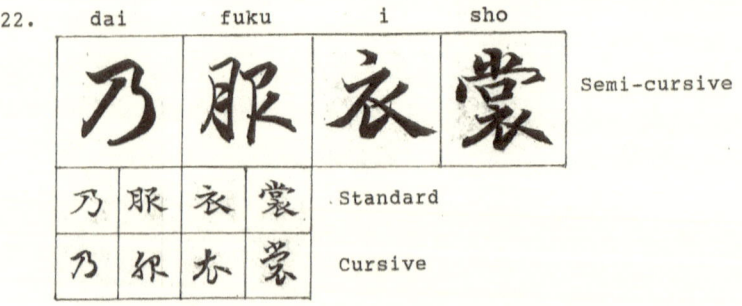

Semi-cursive
Standard
Cursive

People wore clothing for the first time. Kihaku(岐伯 qi bo) created costumes from the beginning legendary.
dai(乃 nǎi)be,so,you,your,therefore, fuku(服 fu)clothes,dress, i(衣 yī)clothing,garment, sho(裳 cháng)skirt(worn in ancient China).

23. sui  i  jo  koku

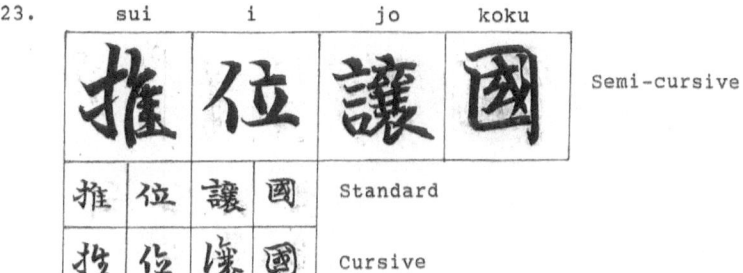

Semi-cursive / Standard / Cursive

The Emperor advocates his throne in favor of the other and offers his country. sui(推 tūi)shove,a mill,elect,hand over, i(位 wèi)place,position,throne, jo(讓 ráng)give away,offer,invite, koku(國 guó)country,nation,state.


24. yu  gu  to  to

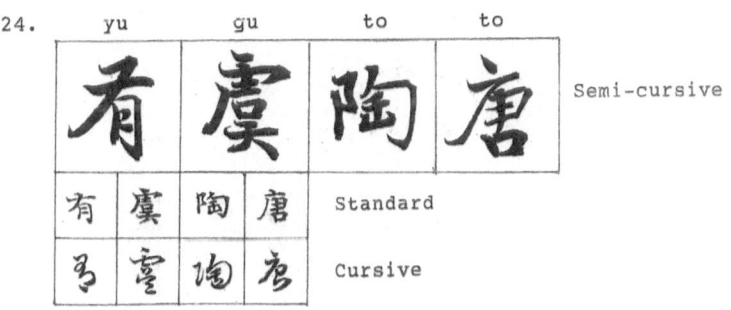

Semi-cursive / Standard / Cursive

Yugu(有虞 yǒu yú) is the capital of Shun(舜 shun) and Toto(陶唐 tao tang) is the capital of Gyo(堯 yao).Shuntei(舜帝 shun di) and Gyotei(堯帝 yao di)'s sons were not intellectual. That caused a lot of trouble for their countries. yu(有 you)have,exist,possess, there is, gu(虞 yu)the name of legendary dynasty founded by Shun(舜 ), the name of a state in the Zhou(周 ) Dynasty,a surname,anxiety, to(陶 táo)pottery,a surname,happy,educate, to(唐 táng)the Tang Dynasty 618 - 907, exaggerative,in vain.

25.

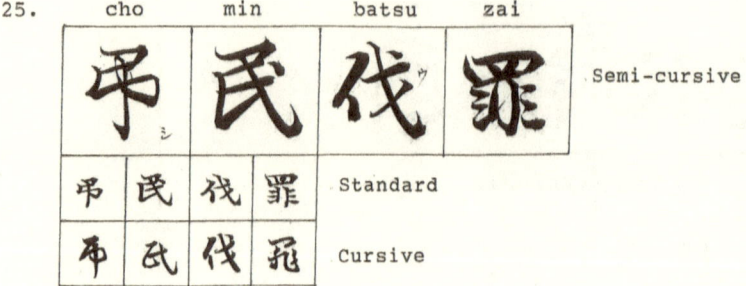

The Emperor held a funeral for his nation and judged the criminal people, cho(吊 diào)hang,lift up,hold a funeral, min(民 min)people, the nation, batsu(伐 fā)cut down,attack,boast about, zai(罪 zùi) crime,fault,pain,hardship.

26

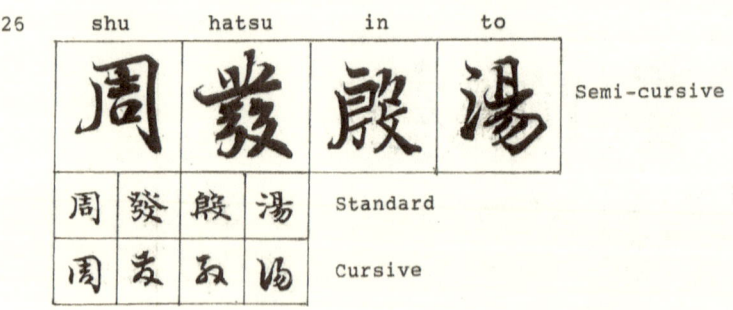

Emperor Hatsu(發 fa = Buo 武王 wu wang) of the Zhōu Dynasty(周 C. 11th century - 256 B.C.) and Emperor Too(湯王 tang wang) of the Ying Dynasty殷 (C. 14th century - 11 century B.C.).
殷

27.

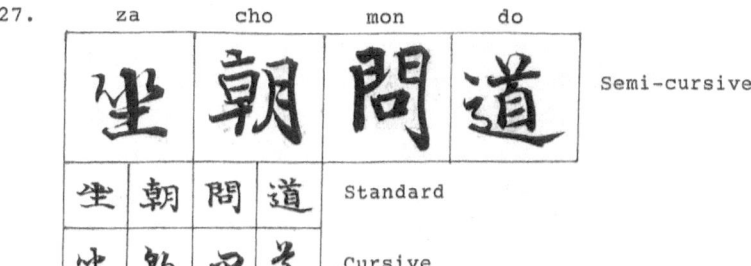

The emperor sit and discuss his deputies about the way of administration at the imperial court. za(坐 zuò)sit,bear, cho(朝 zhāo)every morning,day,imperial court, mon(問 wèn)ask,interrogate, do(道 dào)way,method,principle.

28.

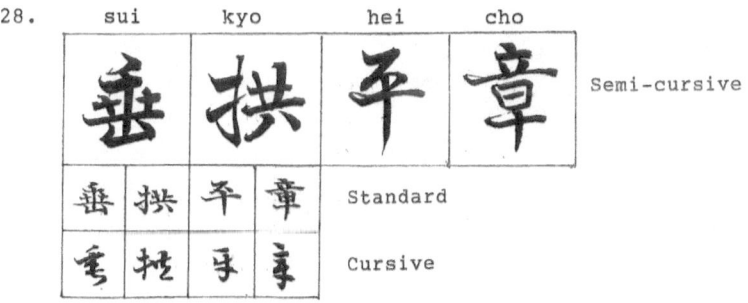

He hangs his clothes, and holds his arms and pacifies.
sui(垂 chuí)hang down,droop, kyo(拱 gǒng)surround,arch,push with the shoulders or head, hei(平 píng)flat,smooth,equal,peaceful, sho(章 zhāng)chapter,section,order,a surname,stamp,medal.

29.

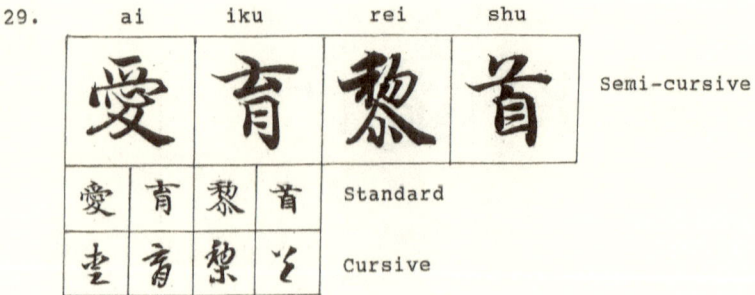

The Emperor brought up the whole people.
ai( 愛 ài)love,like,cherish,treasure, iku( 育 yù)raise,bring up,
rei( 黎 lí)many,lots of, shu( 首 shǒu)head,first,leader,chief.

30.

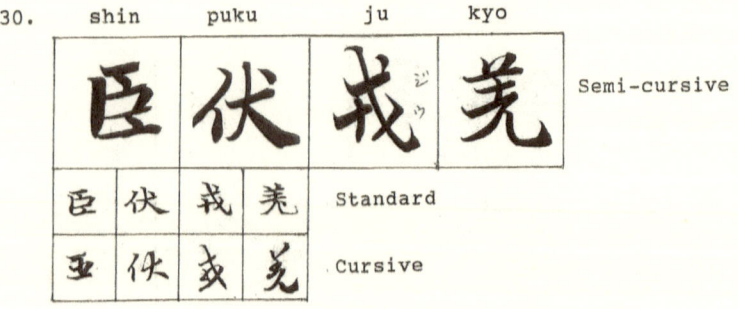

Even the nation of Jukyo( 戎羌 róng qiāng = Ebisu 夷 yí) followed
and respected his virtue. shin( 臣 chén)minister,an official under
a feudal ruler, puku( 伏 fú)lean over,subside,go down,hide,a surname,
ju( 戎 róng)army,military affairs, kyo( 羌 qiāng)the Qiang(Chang)
nationality.

31.

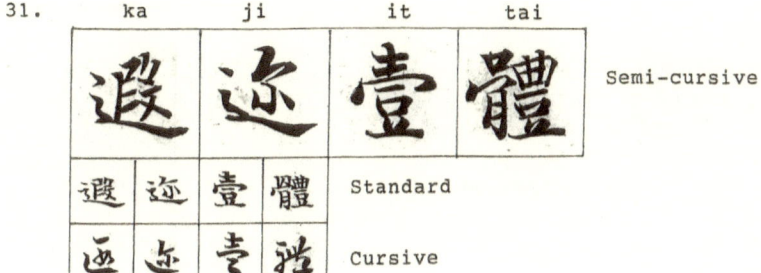

Far and close nations were united into one and followed the government's policy. ka(遐 xiá)far,distant, ji(迩 ěr)near,close, itsu(壹 yī)one(used as the numeral), tai(體 tǐ)body,style,form.

32.

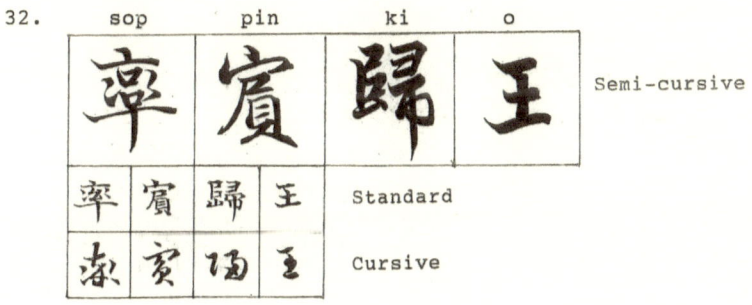

Even cities bordering on the sea obeyed the emperor's order because of his virtue. sotsu(率 shuài)lead,command,obey, bin(賓 bīn)guest, ki(歸 guī)go back to,submit,a aurname.  o(王 wáng)king.

33.   mei     ho     zai     ju

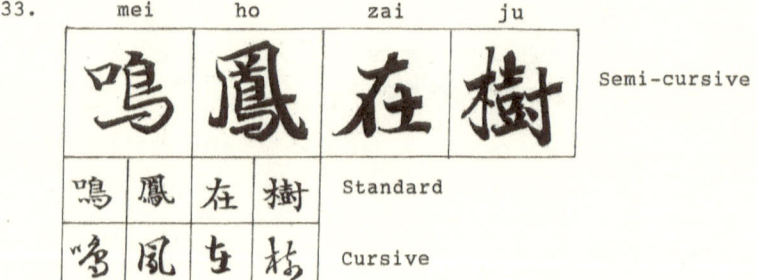

A phoenix sings on the branch of a tree.
It came to mean " World Peace ".   mei(鳴 ming)cry,sing,make a sound,
voice, ho(鳳 fēng)phoenix, hoo(鳳凰 fèng huáng)phoenix.

 zai(在 zài)exist,be alive,be at,lie in,consist in join, ju(樹 shù)
tree,plant,cultivate,set up,     establish,belong to an organization,
(preparation: at,in,or on(a place or time).

34.   haku    ku     shoku    jo

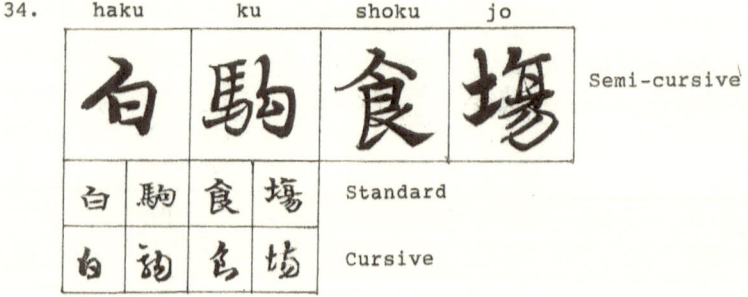

Even a white horse peacefully eats grass at the meadow.
haku(白 bái)white,pure,blank,a surname, ku(駒 ju)colt,foal,
shoku(食 shí)eat,meal,food, jo(場 cháng)meadow,country fair,market.

35.

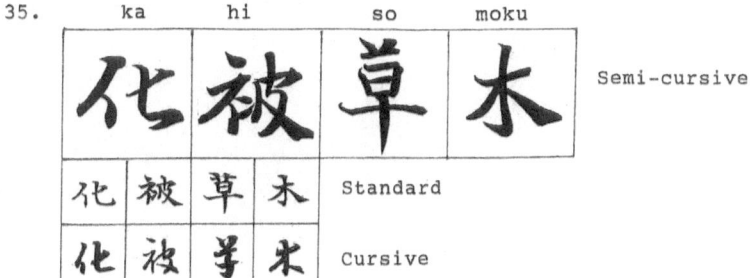

Under the emperor's virtue, trees and grass grow up well.
ka(化 huà)change,transform,melt, hi(被 bèi)quilt,cover with,
so(草 cǎo)grass,cursive script, moku(木 mù)tree,made of wood.


36.

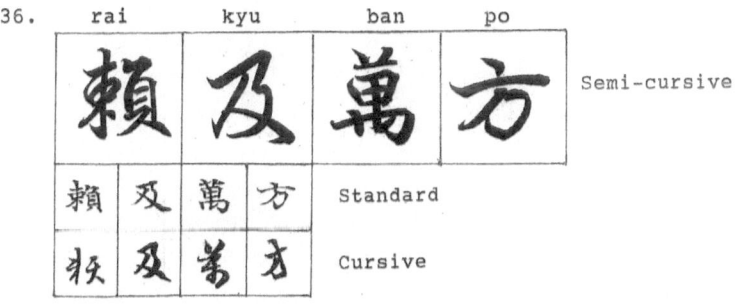

Happiness spreads all over the nations and even outside of the
country. rai(賴 lài) happiness, rely,responsibility,blame,kyu(及 jí)
and,reach,come up to,as well as, ban(萬 wàn)ten thousand,a surname,
po(方 fāng)square,power,direction,place,honest.

37.

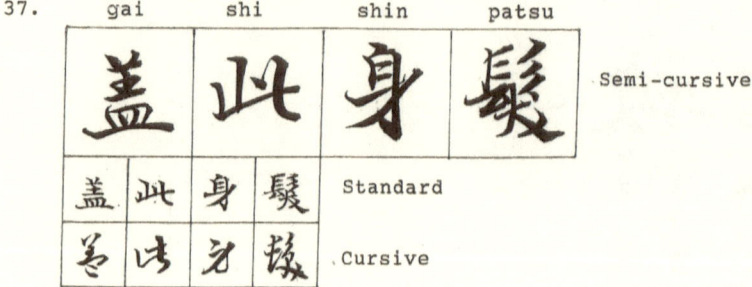

One's whole body was given by his parents.
gai(蓋 gài)lid,cover,shell of a tortoise or crab, shi(此 cǐ)this, here and now, shin(身 shēn)body,life,oneself, patsu(髮 fǎ)hair.


38.

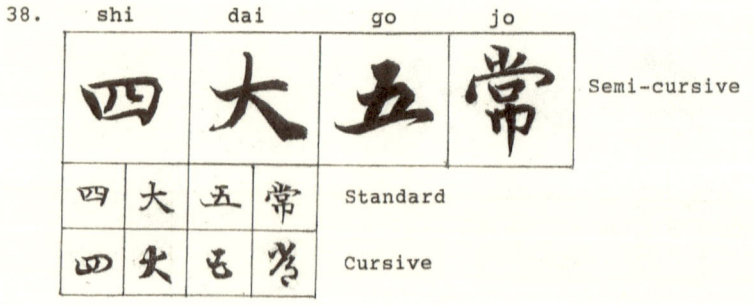

According to the four 四 sì elements are like earth(do 土 tu),water(mizu 水 shui),fire(hi 火 huo) and wind(kaze 風 feng), we live under the five cardinal virtues(gojo 五常 wǔ chang:gorin 五倫 wu lun,gogyo 五行 wu xing),jin(仁 ren mercy,sympathy),gi(義 yi morality),rei(礼 li Rite),chi(智 zhi wisdom), and shin(信 xin trust).Gogyo(五行 wu xing)the five elements are mizu(水 shui water),hi(火 huo fire),ki(木 mu tree),kin(金 jin gold,metal), and tsuchi(土 tu soil).

39.  kyo    i    kiku    yo

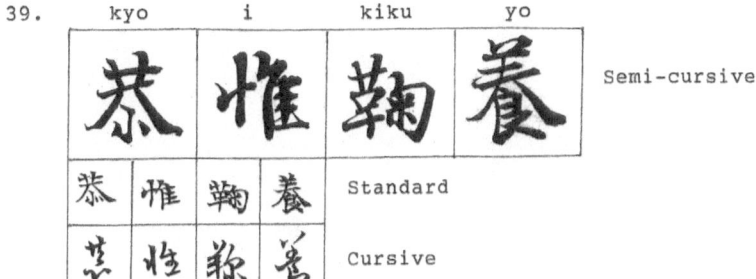

Semi-cursive

Standard

Cursive

Children! Respect your parents and show your gratitude to them for bringing you up. kyo(恭 gōng)respectful, i(惟 wéi)only,thinking, kiku(鞠 jú)bring up,a surname,a ball used in play in ancient time, yo(養 yǎng)support,raise,grow,rest.

40.  ki    kan    ki    sho

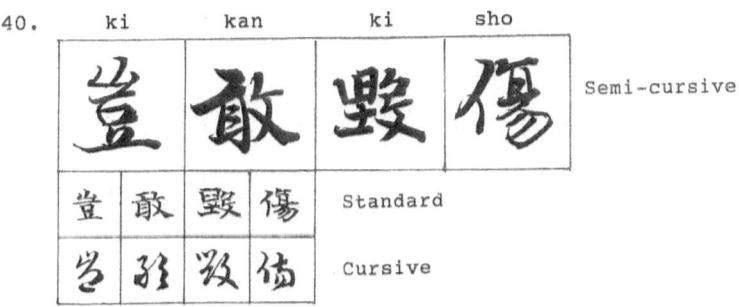

Semi-cursive

Standard

Cursive

Why don't you hurt yourself when you think of your thoughtfulness. ki(豈 qǐ)Oh!, kan(敢 gǎn)bold,dare,afraid,perhaps, ki(毀 huǐ) destroy,ruin,damage, sho(傷 shāng)injury,hurt,hinder.

41.

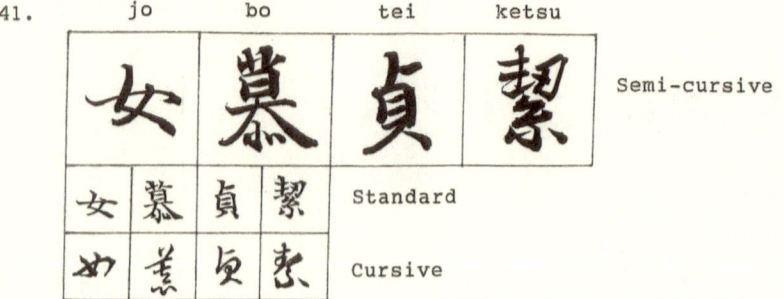

A woman should be chaste(purity).
jo(女 nǚ)woman,daughter,girl, bo(慕 mù)admire,love,adore,tei(貞 zhēn) loyal,faithful,virginity,ketsu(絜 jié)clean.

42.

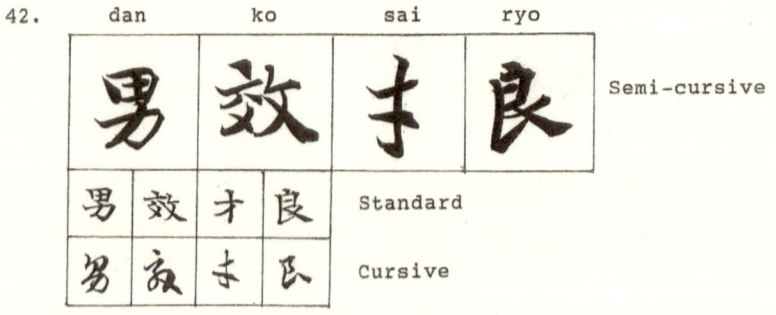

A man follows being well-educated and does a good deed.
dan(男 nán)man,male,son,boy,baron, ko(效 xiào)effect,become,sai(才 cài)ability,talent, ryo(良 liang)good,fine,good people.

43.

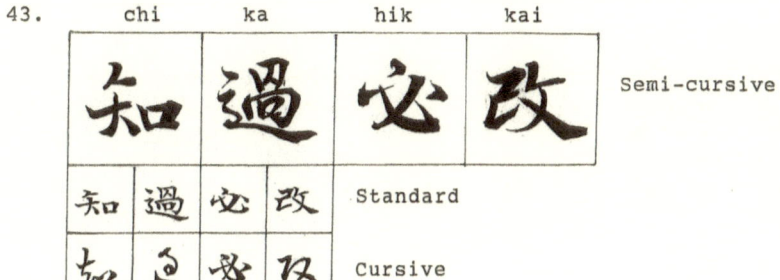

When you find your mistake, correct the error(mistake) immediately.
chi(知 zhī)know,knowledge,administer, ka(過 guò)mistake,pass,fault,
go beyond, hitsu(必 bì)certainly,surely,must, kai(改 gǎi)change,
revise,correct.

44.

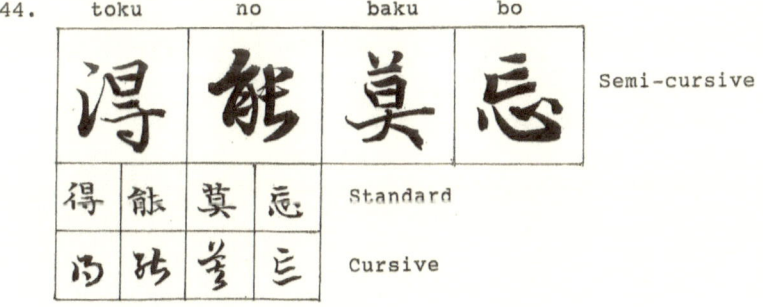

Don't forget to know what is what(reason).
toku( 得 dé)get,obtain,fit,be ready,need, no(能 néng)ability,reason,
baku(莫 mò)do not,no one,nothing,no,a surname, bo(忘 wàng)forget.

45.     bo       dan       hi       tan

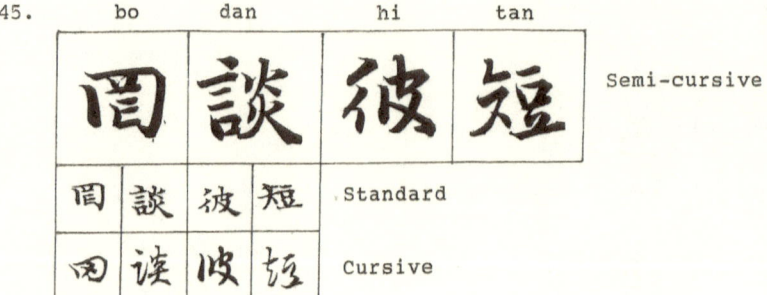

Don't talk about other people's faults.
bo(罔 wang)deceive,do not,without, dan(談 tan)talk,discuss, a surname, hi(彼 bi)the other,another,the other party, tan(短 duan) lack,weak point,fault.

46.     bi       ji       ki       cho

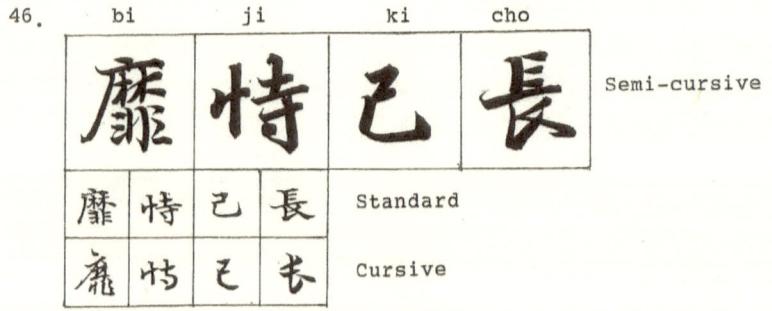

You should not broadcast your merits.
bi(靡 mi)spend,to flutter,bow,wave,waste, ji(恃 shì)rely on,depend on, ki(己ji)oneself,personal, cho(長 cháng)long,strong point, be good at.

47.  shin  shi  ka  fuku

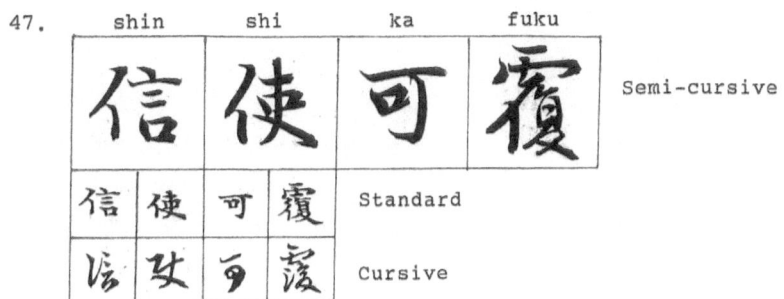

Semi-cursive
Standard
Cursive

You should not betray one's expectations(reliability).
shin(信 xīn)true,real,trust,message,a surname, shi(使 shǐ)use,make,
should,apply,if, ka(可 kě)approve,need,but,about, fuku(覆 fù)cover,
overturn,turn round,answer.

47.  ki  yoku  nan  ryo

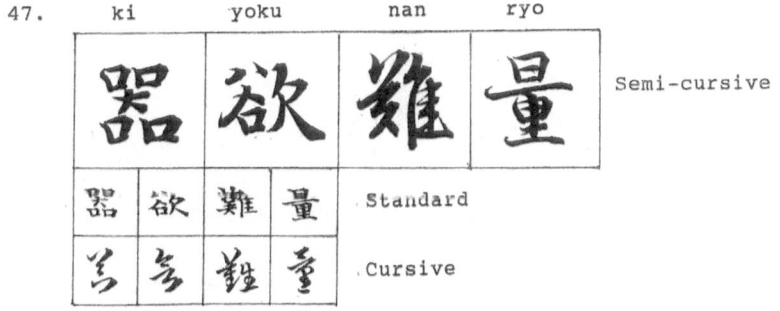

Semi-cursive
Standard
Cursive

Don't show your capacity to others, and you will be respected
by people. ki(器 qì)organ,implement,capacity,talent, yoku(欲 yù)
desire,longing,wish,be about to, nan(難 nán)difficult,hard,bad,
ryo(量 liáng)measure,evaluate,estimate.

49.

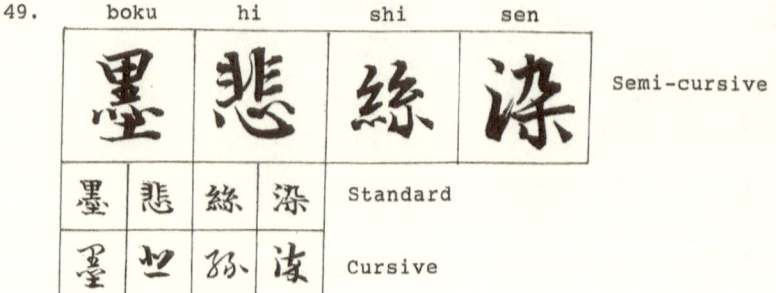

When Bokushi(墨子 mòzǐ or 墨翟 mòdí) saw threads were dyed various colors, he cried they were like one associates with dishonest people(bad friends). boku(墨 mò)Chinese ink,ink stick,pigment,black, a surname, hi(悲 bēi)sad,sorrowful,cry,compassion, shi(絲 sī)silk, a thread,a thread like things, sen(染 rǎn)dye,acqire a bad habit.

50.

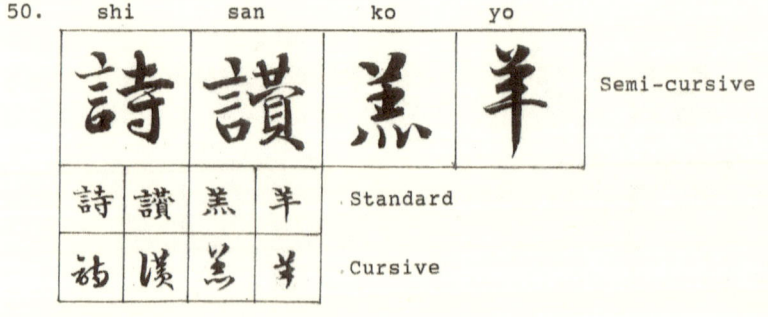

Shi kyo(詩経 shī jīng The Book of Songs) indecated to admire the volume of Koyo(羔羊 gāo yáng). It means Buno(King 文王 wén wáng)'s political policy was excellent. shi(詩 shi)poetry,verse, san(讚 zan)praise,commend, ko(羔 gāo)lamb,kid,fawn, yo(羊 yáng) sheep,a surname.

51.

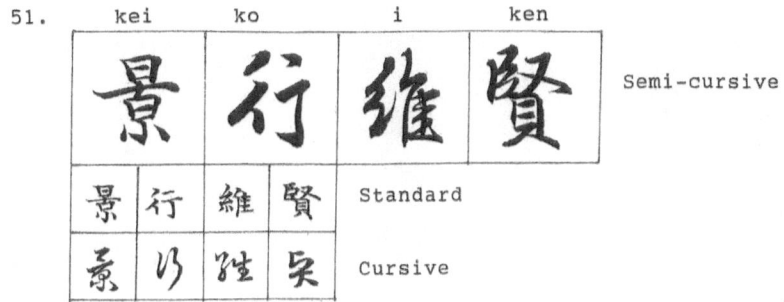

Semi-cursive

Standard

Cursive

One has good deeds. It means the person is wise.
kei(景 jǐng)view,situation,condition,admire,respect, ko(行 xíng)go,
do,conduct,will do, i(維 wéi)tie up,hold together, ken(賢 xián)
wise,virtuous,worthy,a worthy person.


52.

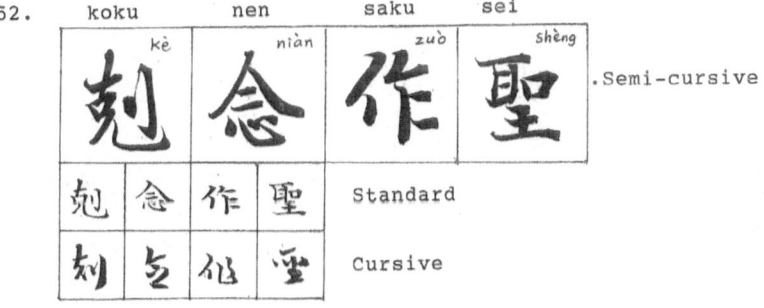

.Semi-cursive

Standard

Cursive

If one keeps that like a holy person's mind,you will be able to
approach the sainthood.This is from the Shokyo(書経 shū jīng)
one of the five classics:1.The Book of Songs(shikyo 詩経 shī jīng)
2.The Book of History(shokyo書経 shū jīng)3.The Book of Changes(
ekikyo 易経yì jīng)4.The Book of Rite(raiki 礼記 lǐ jīng)
5.The Spring and Autumn Annals(shunshu 春秋 chūn qiū):People used
the terms since the Han Dynasty(kan 漢 hàn 206B.C. - 220A.D. under
the Confucianism(jukyo 儒教 rú jiào).The five classics(gokyo 五経
wǔ jīng).

53.   toku   ken   mei   ritsu

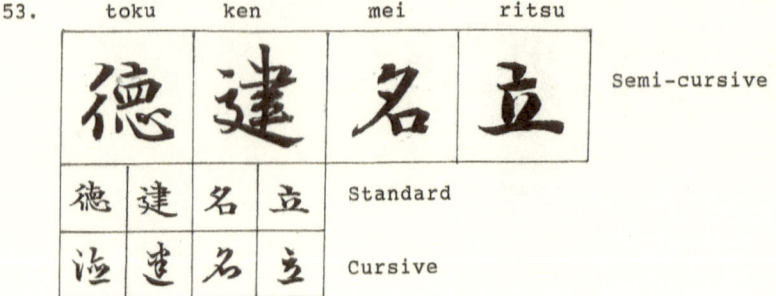

Semi-cursive

Standard

Cursive

If one has virtue, his conduct spreads all over.
toku(德 dé)virtue,mind,heart, ken(建 jiàn)build,stand,set up,found,
mei(名 míng)name,given name,fame,reputation,celebrated, ritsu(立
lì)stand,set,establish,appoint,exist.


54.   kei   tan   kyo   sei

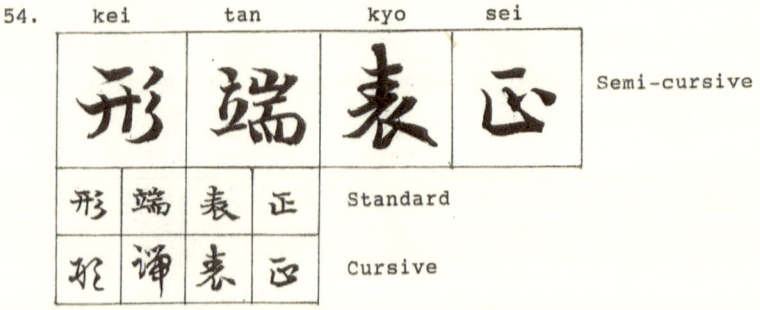

Semi-cursive

Standard

Cursive

Right behavior indicates a good deed.
(from the Book of Rites:raiki 礼記 lǐ jīng).
kei(形 xíng)form,shape,body,appear, tan 端 duān)end,extremity,point,
hyo(表 biǎo)surface,outside,show,model,example,table,list, sei(正
zhèng)straight,right,honest,correct,standard.

55.

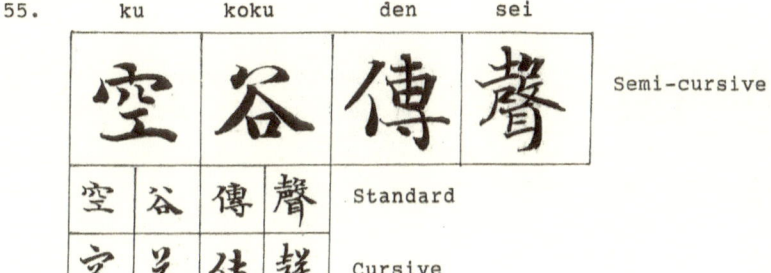

When you raise your voice in the lonely valley, it produces echoes.
ku(空 kōng)empty,hollow,sky,air,in vain, koku(谷 gǔ)valley, den(傳 chuán)pass on,spread,transmit,express, sei(聲 shēng)sound,voice, tone.

56.

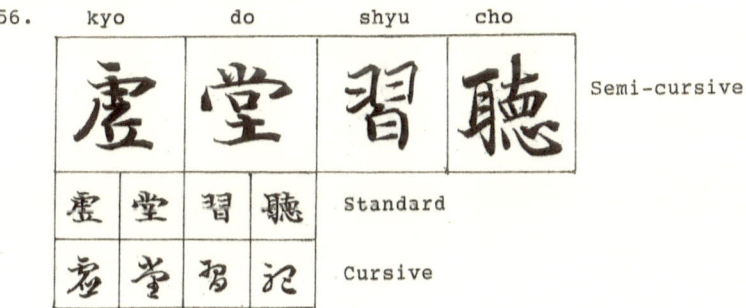

The echoes are like pealing out in the spacious hall. It came to mean " Acquiring virtue is to be rewarded.
kyo(虛 xū)emptiness,void,empty,humble, do(堂 táng)the main room of a house,a hall,old court of law, shu(習 xí)exercise,review,habit, cho(聽 tīng)listen,hear,obey,heed.

57.

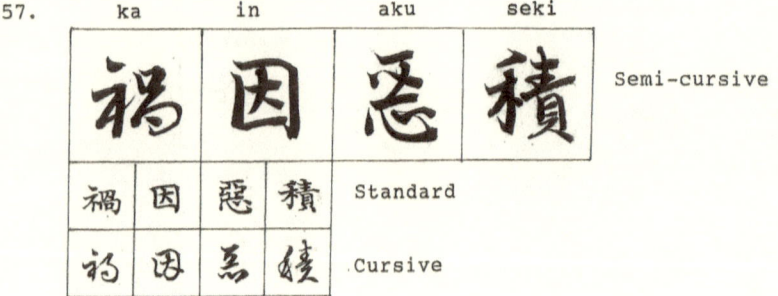

Misfortune is caused by wrong-doing.
ka(禍 huò)misfortune,ruin, in(因 yīn)carry on,cause,reason, aku(悪 è)evil, seki(積 jī)a mass,store up,accumulate.

58.

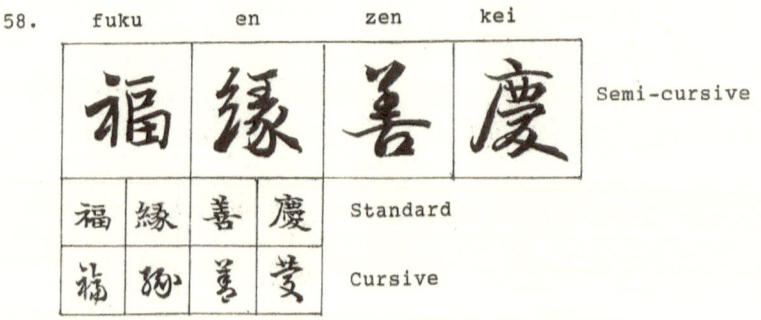

Good fortune related to good conduct.
fuku(福 fú)good fortune,happiness, en(縁 yuán)reason,edge,predestined relationship, zen(善 shàn)good,virtuius,be good at, kei(慶 qìng) celebrate,congratulate,a surname.

59.

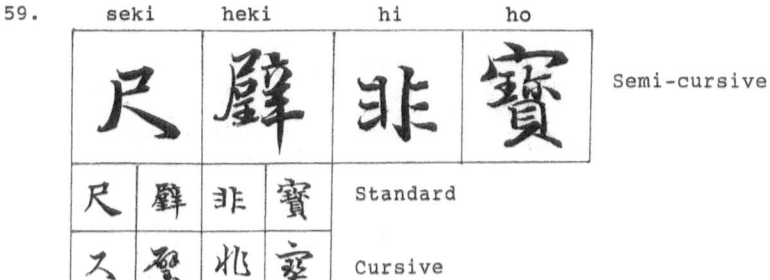

One foot long sphere is very rare, but it is not precious.
seki(尺 chǐ)a traditional unit of length,ruler, heki(璧 bì)a round flat piece of jade with a hole in its center,hi( 非 fēi)wrong,non-,be not,wrongdoing, ho(寶 bǎo)treasure, precious.

60.

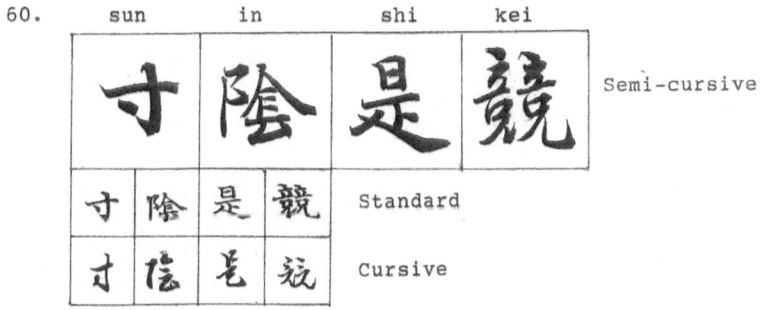

One makes use of every spare moment to study.
sun(寸 cùn)a traditional unit of length,very short,small, in(陰 yīn)yin in Chinese thought,the feminine,north of a hill or south of a river

Yin)yin in Chinese thought,the feminine,north of a hill or south of a river,a surname, shi(是 shì)this,that,correct,yes, kei(競 jìng) compete,contend,vie.

61.    shi    fu    ji    kun

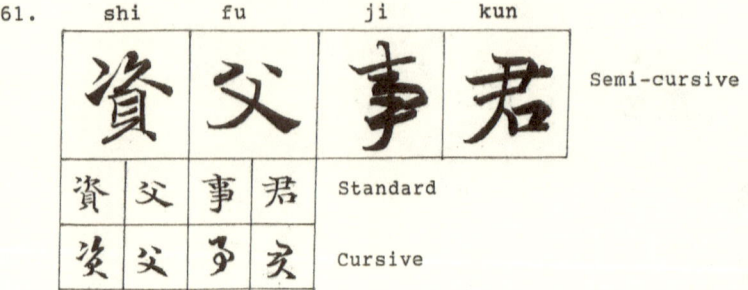

Semi-cursive

Standard

Cursive

Serve your monarch respectfully as well as your parents.
shi(資 zi)money,provide,a surname,natural ability, fu(父 fù)father,
ji(事 shi)matter,work,serve,be engaged in,accident, kun(君 jūn)
you,monarch,supreme ruler,sir.


62.    etsu    gen    yo    kei

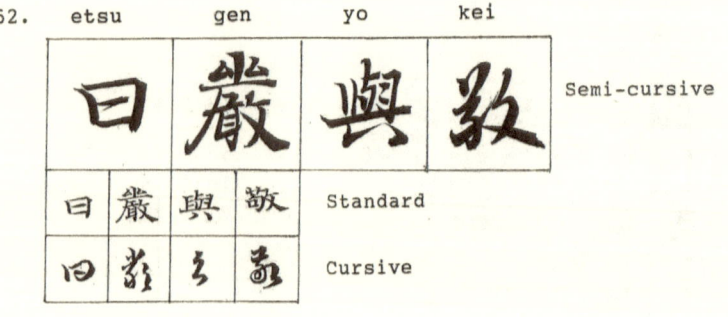

Semi-cursive

Standard

Cursive

Allegiance and being good to your parents.
Kokyo(孝教 xiao jing) The Book of Final Duty by Soshi(曾子 zeng zi
= Sosan 曾参  zeng can 505B.C. - ?).
  Soshin

etsu(曰  yuē)say,call name, gen(嚴 yán)tight,strict,severe,father,
stern, yo(與 yǔ)give,offer,grant,help,support, kei(敬 jìng)respect,
offer politely.

67.

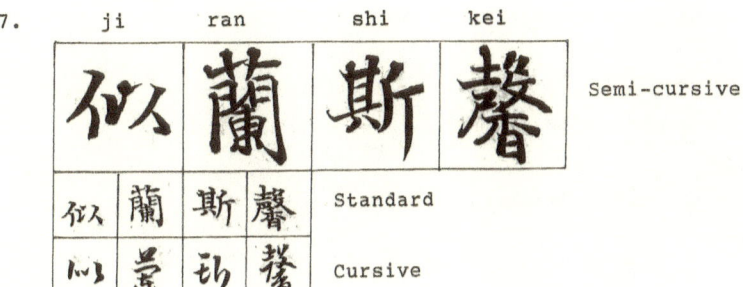

The way of loyalty and filial piety is similar, like the fragrance of a orchid or evergreen pine tree. ji(似 si)similar, ran(蘭 lán) lily magnolia,orchid, shi(斯 si)this,thus, kei(馨 xīn)fragrance, the sweet smell of burning incense.

68.

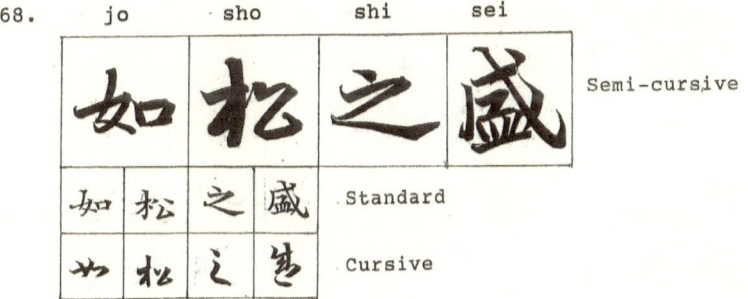

It means vigorous like a pine tree. jo(如 rú)like,as,if,such as, for instance, sho(松 sōng)pine tree,a surname,relax,soft, shi(之 zhī)go,this,of,leave for, sei(盛 sei)fill,ladle,contain,hold.
  chéng

69.

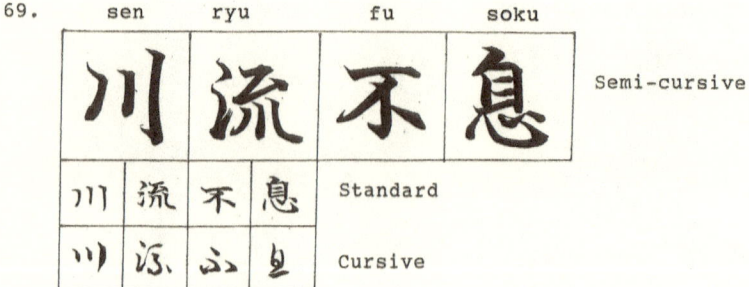

A stream never stops. The way of filial duty should be continuous actions. sen(川 chuān)river,plain, ryu(流 liú)moving from place to place, fu(不)not,not want to, soku(息 xī)breath,stop,rest,news.
bù

70.

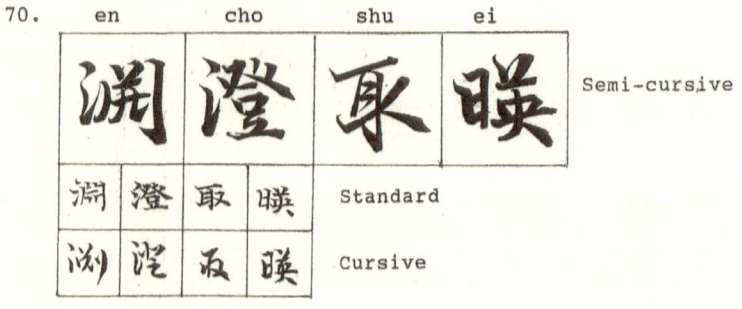

Your shadow is reflected in the clear water of the deep pool. The clear water means sincerity. The Book of Wai Nan Shi(淮南子 huái nan zi) 173 - 122B.C.  en(淵 yuān)a deep pool, cho(澄 chéng) clear of water or air,clarify, shu(取 qǔ)take,get,adopt,aim at, ei(暎 yìng)reflect,mirror,shine.

63.

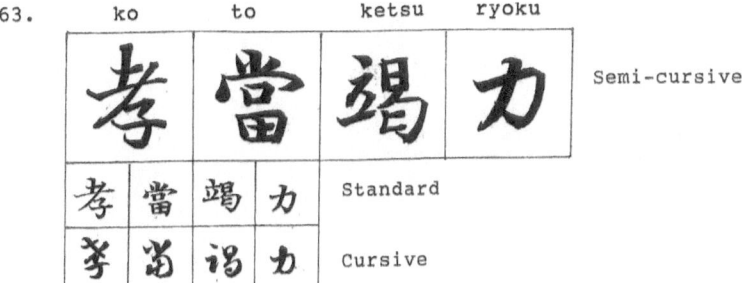

Final duty is serve your parents with all one's might.
ko(孝 xiào)filial, to(當 dāng)equal,ought to,must,accept, ketsu(竭 jié)use up,exhaust, ryoku(力 li)power,strength,ability.

64.

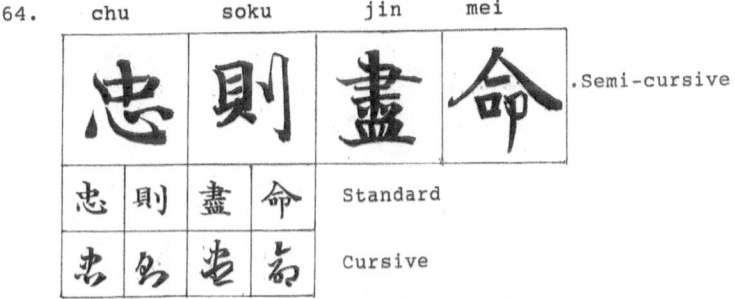

A monarch is pledged by his subordinates. The monarch's orders are followed by his subordinates. Rongo(論語 lun yu)The Analects of Confucius. chu(忠 zhōng)loyal,honest, soku(則 zé)standard,norm,rule, jin(盡 jin)finished,use up,try one's best, mei(命 ming)life,lot,fate.

65.  rin   shin   ri   haku

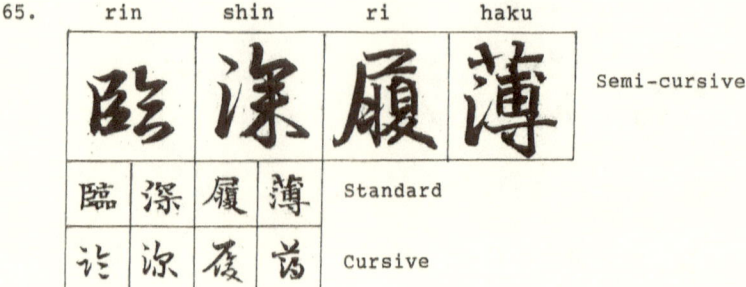

Semi-cursive
Standard
Cursive

Respect your parents. It is like that you step on the thin ice carefully or get into the depths. rin(臨 lín)overlook,be present, just before, shin(深 shēn)deep,depth,penetrating,intimate,dark, night,greatly, ri(履 lǔ)shoe,tread on,walk on, carry out,footstep, haku(薄 báo)thin,light,lacking in warmth.

66.  shuku   ko   on   sei

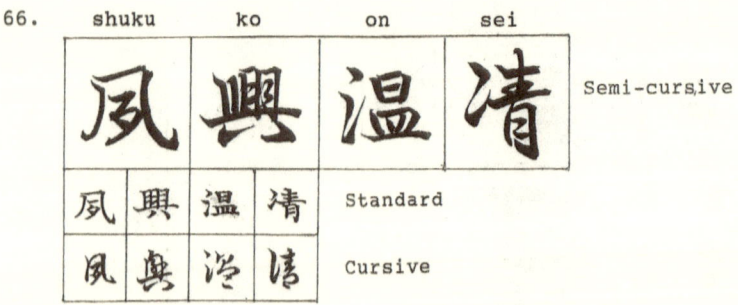

Semi-cursive
Standard
Cursive

Take care of your parents carefully. Get up early in the morning. Keep them warm during the winter time and make them cool in summer. Raiki(礼記 li jing) The Book of Rites. shuku(夙 sù)early in the morning,old,, ko(興 xing)get up,start,prosper, on(温 wēn)warm, temperature,a surname, sei(清 jing)cool,cold,coldhearted.

71.

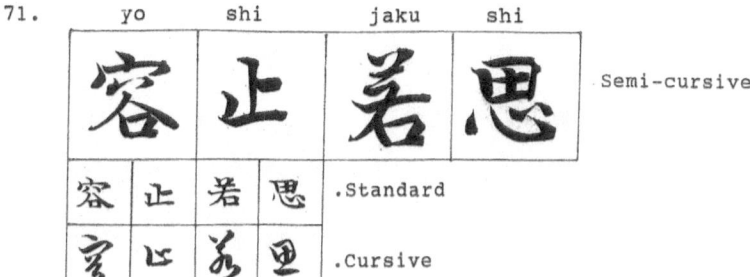

Think about your behavior and be calm.
yo(容 róng)hold,contain,permit,allow,perhaps,a surname, shi(止 zhǐ)
stop,to,till,only, jaku(若 ruò)as if,like,you, shi(思 si)think,
consider,long for,thought,thinking.

72.

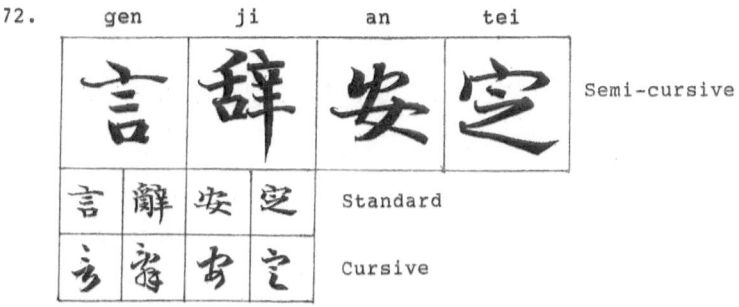

Stabilize your expressions without excitment. gen(言 yán)speech,
say,talk,word,a surname, ji(辭 cí)diction,phraseology,a form of
classical poetry, an(安 ān)peaceful,at ease,safe,secure,place in
suitable position, tei(定 dìng)clam,stable,fix,settled,established.

73.   toku   sho   sei   bi

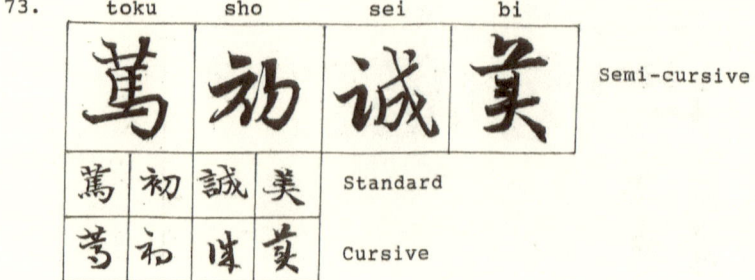

Semi-cursive
Standard
Cursive

First devote the cultivation of the mind,
toku(篤 dǔ)sincere,earnest,serious,critical, sho(初 chū)first,
the beginning of,the early part of,for the first time,elementary,
rudimentary,a surname, sei(誠 chéng)sincere,honest,actually,real,
bi(美 měi)beautiful,pretty,very satisfactory,short for bikoku(美国
meiguo) or bishu(美州 meizhōu).


74.   shin   shyu   gi   rei

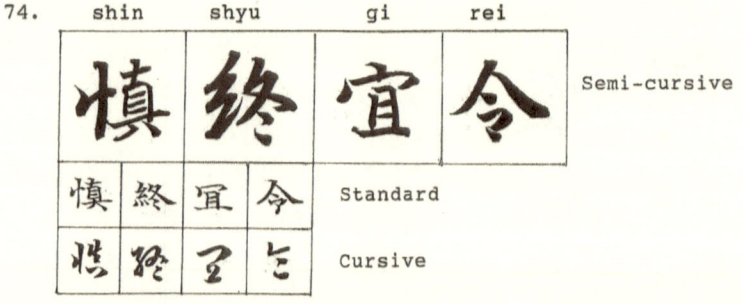

Semi-cursive
Standard
Cursive

and do your best at the end of the project,then you will be able to
get a good result. shin(慎 shèn)careful,cautious, shu(终 zhong)end,
finish,die,whole,entire,all, gi(宜 yí)suitable,appropriate,should,
rei(令 ling)order,command,good,excellent,season,decree.

75.  ei   gyo   sho   ki

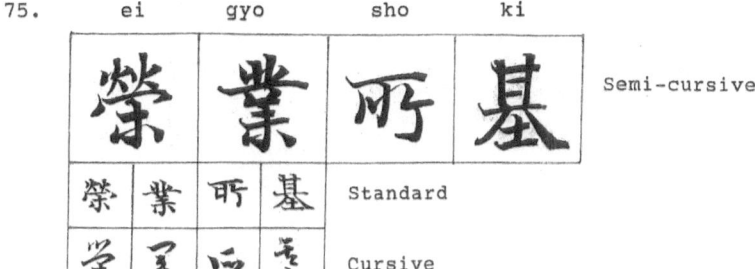

Semi-cursive
Standard
Cursive

Correct your errors and keep a right reed. It is a basic way of succeeding in life. In short, it means to take a honorable position.
ei(榮 róng)grow, luxuriantly,honour,flourishing, gyo(業 yè)trade, industry,occupation,profession,job,Buddhism karma, sho(所 suǒ)place, point,what,department(office), ki(基 jī)base,foundation,key,basic, main,essential.

76.  seki   jin   mu   kei

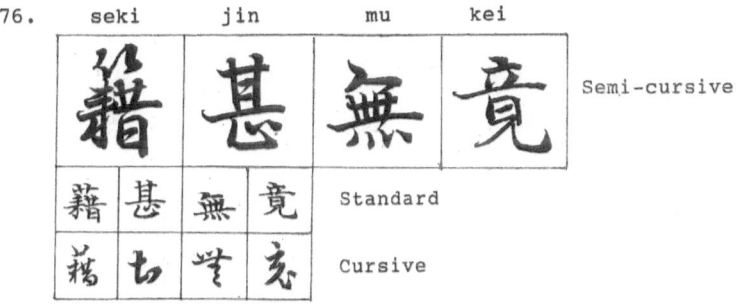

Semi-cursive
Standard
Cursive

Your honor is unlimited, it will live forever.
seki(藉 jí)book,record,roll,home town,birthplace,membership, jin(甚 shèn)very,extremely,more than,whatever, mu(無 wú)nothing, not have,without,not, kei(竟 jìng)finish,complete,have the impudence.

77.

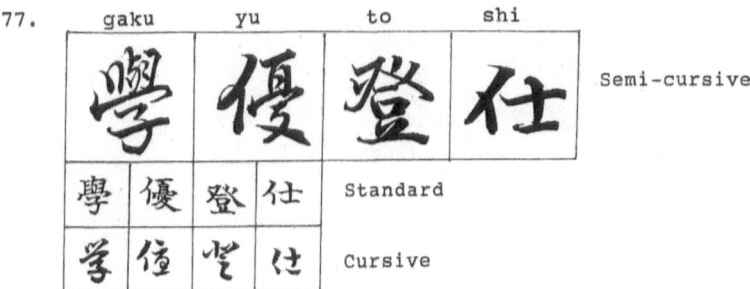

If one's study is excellent, he will be able to work for the government office. gaku(學 xué)study,learn,imitate,knowledge, yu(優 yōu)excellent,actor,actress, to(登 dēng)ascend,scale,record, step on,enter,put on,publish, shi(仕 shì)be an official.


78.

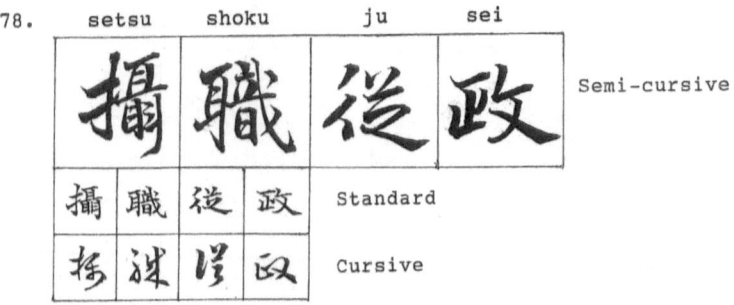

Then he will get a very important position there, and follow the national administration.

setsu(攝 shè)absorb,assimilate,shoot,take a photo of,conserve one's health,act for, shoku(職 zhí)duty,job,post,because of, ju(從 cóng) follow,obey,comply with,join,follower,in a certain manner,secondary, sei(政 zhèng)politics,political affairs.

79.

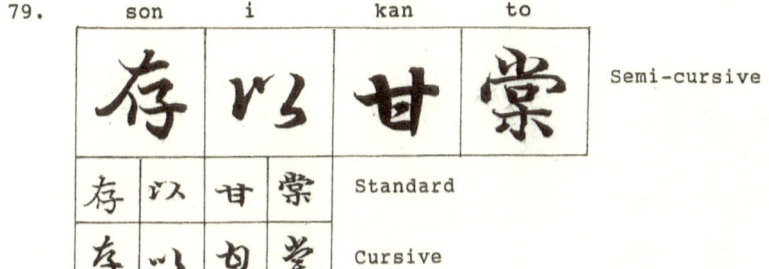

The stateman under the birchleaf pear tree listened to the common people's complaints peacefully, thereafter the people accepted the man's virtue. son(存 cún)exist,live,store,keep,accumulate,check, i(以 yǐ)with,by means of,at,on,because of,according to, kan(甘 gān) sweet,pleasant,willingly,a surname, to(棠 táng)birchleaf pear.

80.

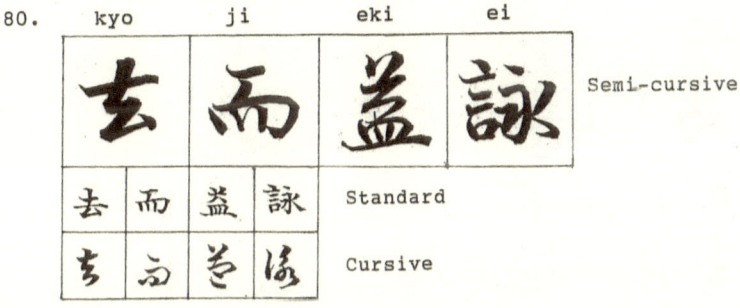

Even after he passed away, they never cut the tree. And the common people admired him in their poems. kyo(去 qù)go,send there,remove, ji(而 ér)and,as well as,so that,in order to, eki(益 yì)benefit, profit,advantage, ,ei(詠 yǒng)chant,express,narrate in poetic form.

81.

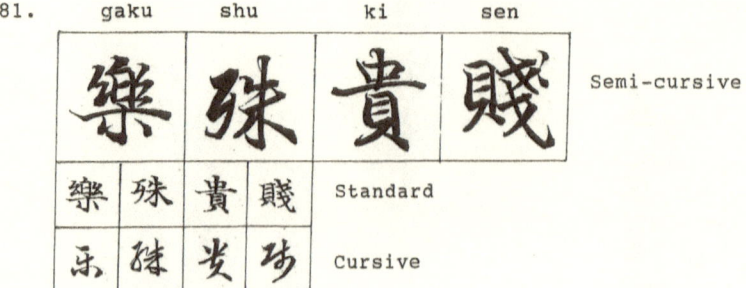

The number of music lovers depended on the class(upper or lower class). raku(樂 lè)happy,joyful,be glad to, shu(殊 shū)different, very much,really, ki(貴 gùi)noble,expensive,costly,valuable,dear, sen(賤 jiàn)low-priced,inexpensive,lowly.


82.

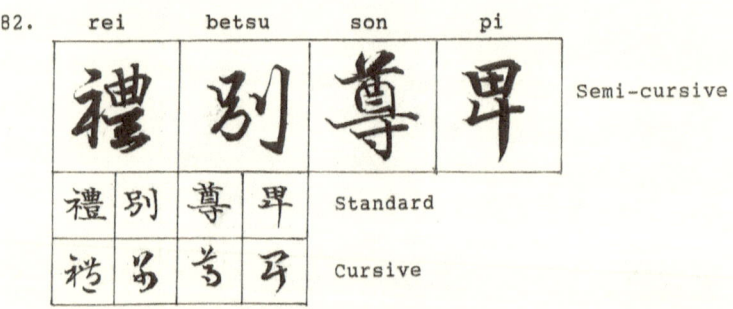

The ceremonies like weddings or funerals are separated into the upper or lower classes. rei(禮 lǐ)ceremony,rite,manner,gift, betsu(別 bié)leave,part,other,another,change,distinguish, son(尊 zūn)senior,respect,honour,your, pi(卑 bēi)low,humble,modest,inferior.

83.     sho      wa      ka      boku

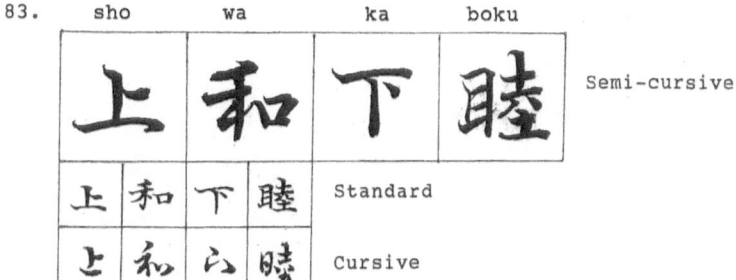

The upper class people behave peacefully to common people, they follow the master. sho(上 shàng)above,upward,first,last,former, wa(和 hé)gentle,mild,kind,peace,a surname, ka(下 xià)below,under, lower,next, boku(睦 mù)peaceful,harmonious.

84.      fu      sho      fu      zui

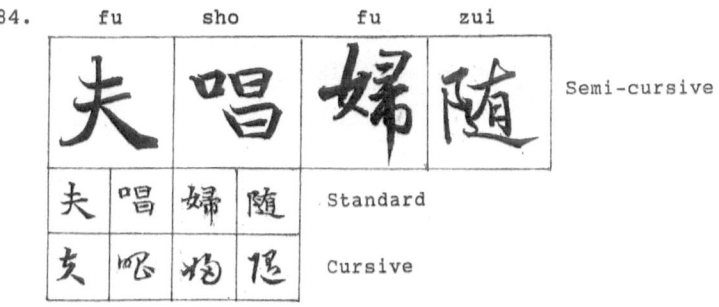

If one's husband leads his wife nicely, she will be able to follow him. This is the way of keeping a good relationship between husband and wife. fu(夫 fū)husband,labourer,man, sho(sing,call,cry,a song 唱), fu(婦 fù)woman,married woman,wife, zui(隨 suí)the Sui Dynasty 581-618, follow,look like,along with,resemble.

85.

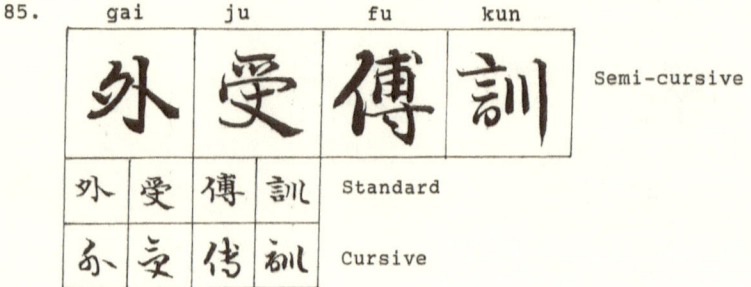

A boy at age 8 follows instruction from a teacher outside.
gai(外 wài)outside,other,foreign,external,class,besides,in addition,
ju(受 shòu)receive,accept,suffer,bear,be pleasant, fu(傅 fù)teach,
kun(訓 xùn)instruct,teachings,model,example,critical explanation.

86.

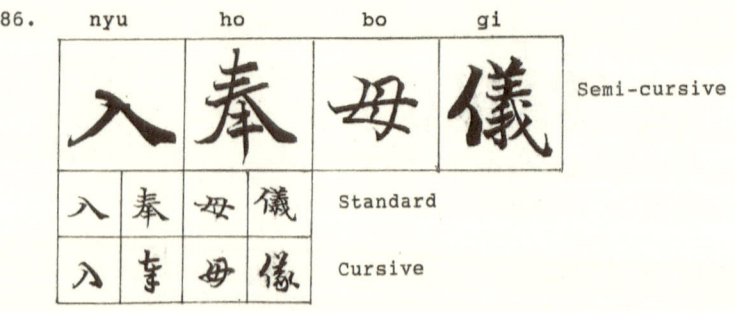

A girl at age 10 stays at home and follows her mother's advice.
  ( This is the institution in ancient China. )
nyu(入 rù)go into,enter,join,income,agree with, ho(奉 fèng)give,
  receive,esteem,attend to, bo(母 mǔ)mother,female, gi(儀 yí)ceremony,
  bearing,gift,appearance,present,instrument.

87    sho    ko    haku    shuku

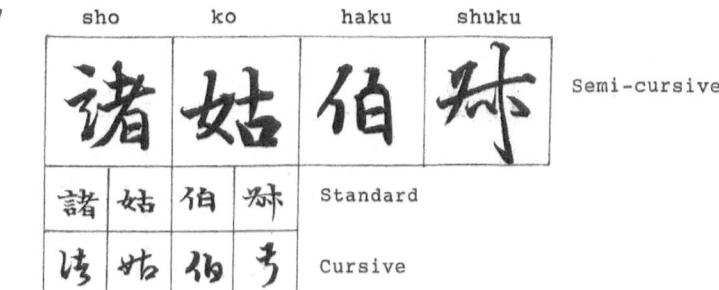

Semi-cursive

Standard

Cursive

When you respect your uncle and aunt like your parents,
sho(諸 zhū)all,various,a surname, ko(姑 gū)aunt,husband's mother
or sister,father's sister,tentatively,for the moment, haku(伯 bó)
father's elder brother,uncle,the eldest among brothers,earl,
shuku(叔 shú)father's younger brother,uncle,the third among brothers.

88.   yu    shi    hi    ji

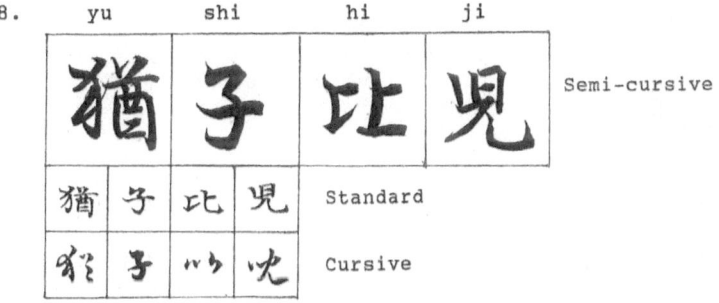

Semi-cursive

Standard

Cursive

they will take care of you like their children. yu(猶 yóu)just as,
like,still, shi(子 zi)son,child,person,you,young,tender,copper,
copper coin,small, hi(比 bi)compare,is likened to,compete,match,
ji(兒 ér)child,youngster,youth.

89.  ko    kai    kei    tei

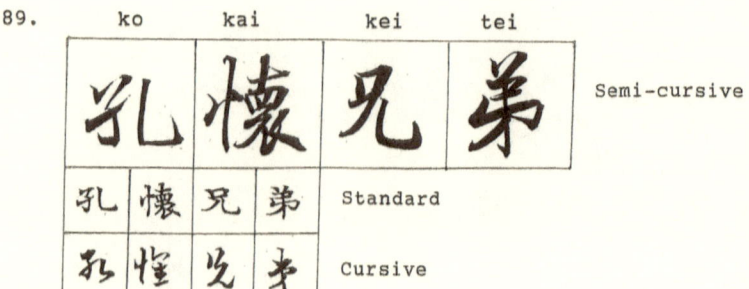

Semi-cursive

Standard

Cursive

Brothers must show their affection for each other.
ko(孔 ko)hole,opening,a surname,very, kai(懷 huai)mind,keep in mind,
cherish,think of, kei(兄 xiōng)elder brother,elder male relative of
the same generation, tei(弟 di)younger brother.
孔 Kǒng

90.  do    ki    ren    shi

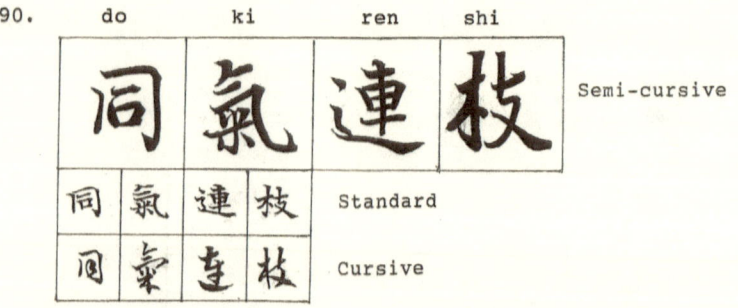

Semi-cursive

Standard

Cursive

Because brothers are like branches of a tree.
do(同 tóng)same,alike,similar, ki(氣 qi)gas,air,breath,smell,odour,
manner,spirit, ren(連 lián)link,join,connect,continuously,including,
shi(枝 zhi)branch,twig.

91.

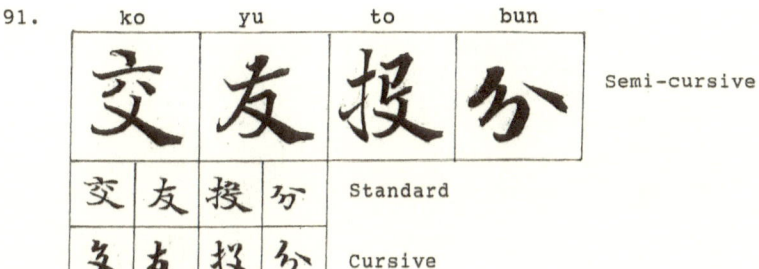

When one associates with a friend, he needs congeniality.
ko(交 jiāo)associate with,friend,hand over,give up,cross,reach,
yu(友 yǒu)friend,friendly, to(投 tóu)throw,fling,put in,project,
send,deliver,hurl, bun(分 fēn)divide,separate,part,distinguish,
fraction,one tenth,minute.

92.

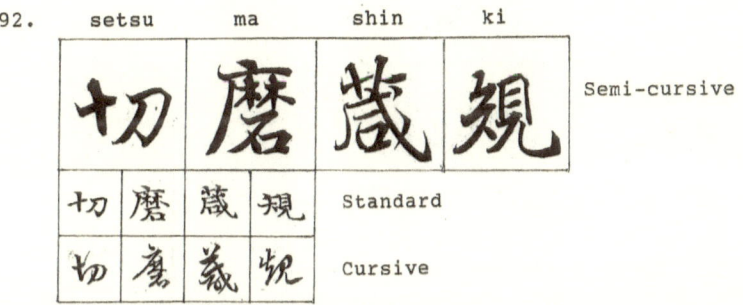

Choose honest people, and study hard, also exercise self-control
strictly, setsu(切 qiē)cut,slice, ma(磨 mó)rub,wear,polish,grind,
worry,trouble, shin(箴 zhēn)admonish,exhort, ki(規 guī)regulation,
rule,admonish,plan.

93.     jin     ji     in     soku

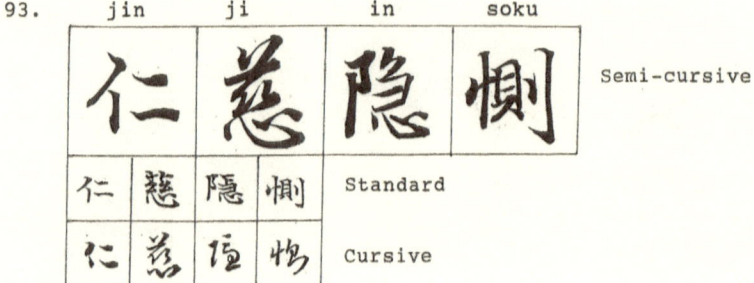

One must have thoughtfulness and virtue with blessing.
jin(仁 rén)kindheartedness,sensitive, ji(慈 cí)kind,loving,mother,
in(隱 yīn)hidden from view,dormant,lurking, soku(惻 cè)sorrowful,
insoku(隱惻 yīn cè)sympathize.


94.     zo     ji     futsu     ri

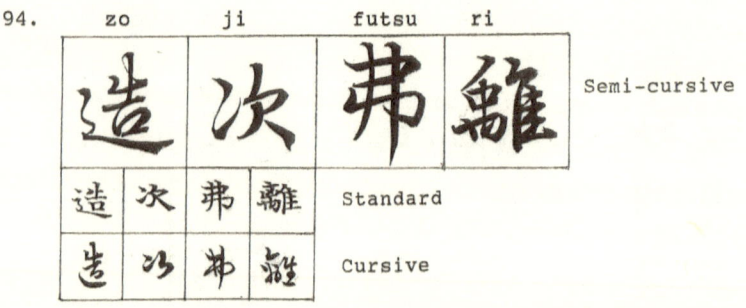

When you find one's agonies, comfort and help the person.
Don't forget these kinds of feelings all the time.
zo(造 zào)make,build,create,invent, ji(次 cì)order,next,place in
a sequence,second, futsu(弗 fú)not, ri(離 lí)leave,from,without,
be away from.

95.    setsu    gi    ren    tai

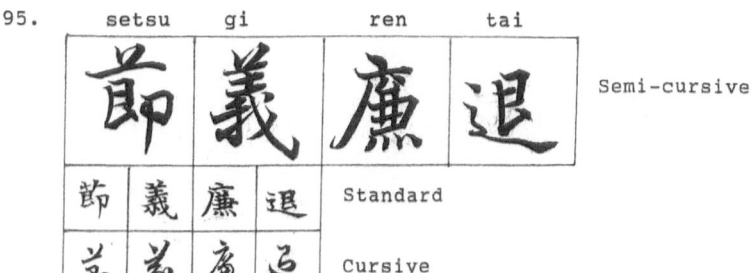

Semi-cursive

Standard

Cursive

One must have integrity and honesty. In addition, one also must be modest. (One keeps his fidelity strictly.)
setsu(節 jié)joint,knot,division,part,section,moral integrity,
gi(義 yì)meaning,justice,relationship,significance,equitable,
ren(廉 lián)honest and clean,low-priced,cheap, a surname, tai(退 tùi)move back,retreat,remove,withdraw,fade,return.


96.    ten    pai    hi    ki

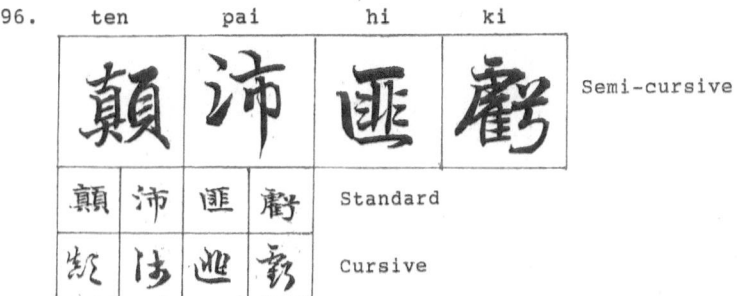

Semi-cursive

Standard

Cursive

Don't lack these manners, even for a moment.
ten(顛 diān)crown of the head,top,fall,turn over, pai(沛 pèi)copious, abundant, tenpai(顛沛 diān pèi)a moment, hi(匪 fěi)not,bandit, robber, ki(虧 kūi)lose money,have a deficit,fortunately,deficient.

97. sei sei jo itsu

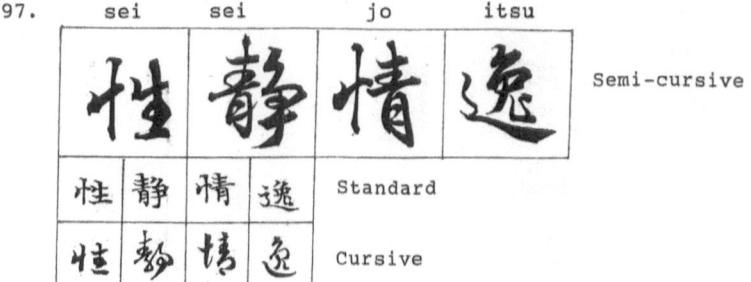

Semi-cursive / Standard / Cursive

A person of fine and calm character has also peaceful in his mind.
sei(性 xing)nature,character,sex,disposition, sei(静 jing)still,
quiet, jo(情 qing)feeling,affection,love,passion,sexual passion,
itsu(逸 yi)ease,leisure,escape,flee,excel,be lost.


98. shin do shin hi

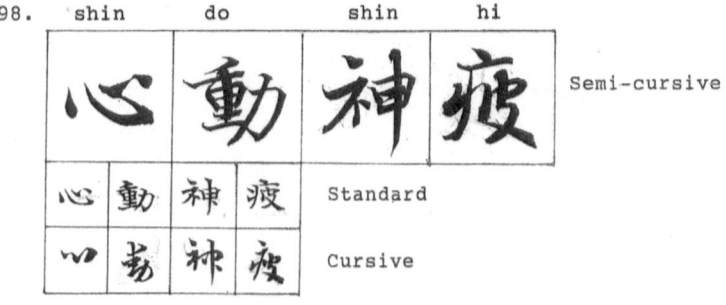

Semi-cursive / Standard / Cursive

On the other hand, if the person is of unstable mind, his behavior
is careless and easy to get tired of spiritually.
shin(心 xin)heart,mind,feeling,center,core, do(動 dòng)move,change,
act,stir,alter,touch,frequently,easily, shin(神 shén)god,deity,
supernatural,magical,expression, hi(疲 pí)tired,exhausted,weary.

99.   shu      shin     shi      man

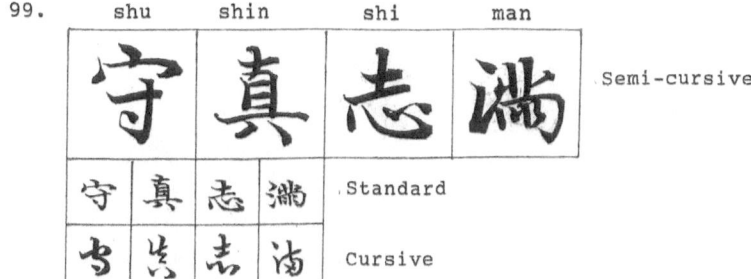

Semi-cursive

Standard

Cursive

A person who is looking for his own way becomes full of ambition.
shu(守 shǒu)guard,defend,keep watch,observe, shin(真 zhēn)true,real,
,clear,unmistakable, shi(志 zhì)will,ideal,measure,keep in mind,
man(满 mǎn)full,filled,packed,fill,expire,perfectly,satisfied,quite.


100.  chiku    butsu     i        i

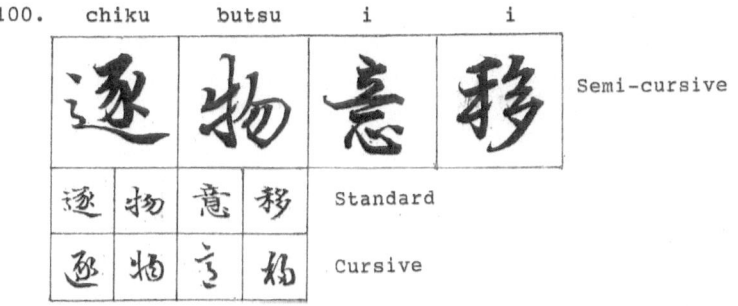

Semi-cursive

Standard

Cursive

But when one wants other things, one's mind will be unstable.
chiku(逐 zhú)pursue,chase,one by one,expel, butsu(物 wù)thing,
matter,content, i(意 yì)meaning,idea,thought,wish,intention,
i(移 yí)move,remove,change,alter.

101. ken    ji    ga    so

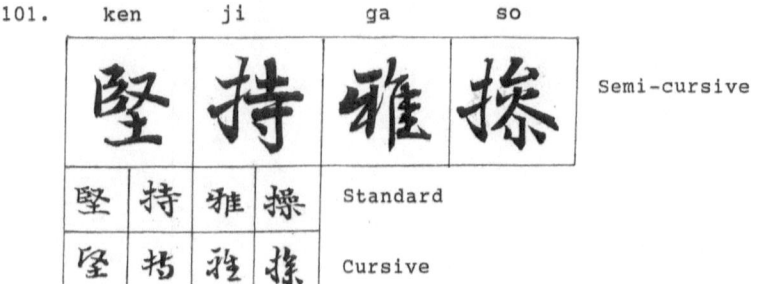

Semi-cursive
Standard
Cursive

A man holds fast to his beliefs and virtue,
ken(堅 jiān)hard,solid,firm,strong,firmly, ji(持 chí)hold,grasp,
ga(雅 yǎ)elegant,   so(操 cāo)grasp,hold,do,operate,drill,exercise,
conduct,behavior.


102. ko    shaku    ji    bi

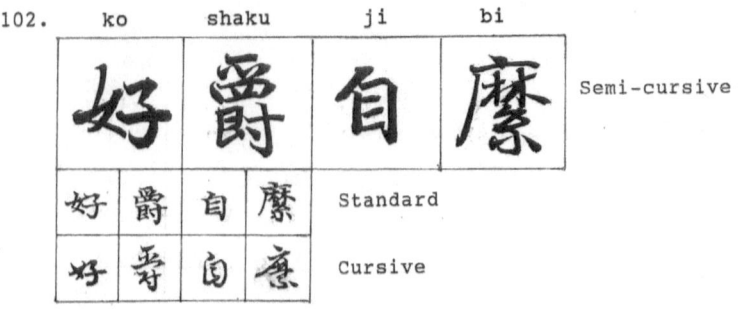

Semi-cursive
Standard
Cursive

thereafter he will be able to take the higher position naturally.
ko(好 hǎo)good,fine,nice,kind,friendly,get well,be ready,
shaku(爵 jué)the rank of nobility,peerage, ji(自 zì)self,oneself,
bi(縻 mí)bind,yoke.

103.    to    yu    ka    ka

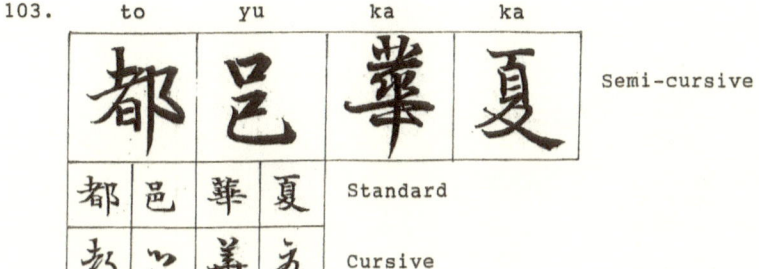

Semi-cursive

Standard

Cursive

Our country's big cities.
to(都 dǒu)all,even,already,capital,big city, yu(邑 yì)town,city,
ka(華 huá)splendid,magnificent,flourishing,best part,China,cream,
ka(夏 xià)summer,the Xia Dynasty C. 21st - 16th century B.C.
kaka(華夏  hua xia)China.


104.    to    zai    ji    kei

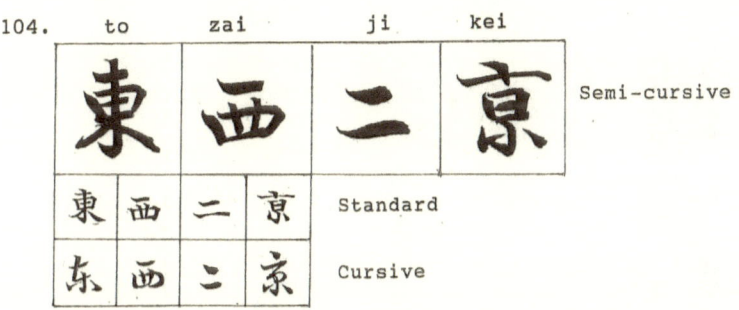

Semi-cursive

Standard

Cursive

In our nation, there are two big cities like capitals,
Rakuyo(洛陽  luo yang) in the east and Choan(長安 chang an)
in the west. to(東 dōng)east,host,master,owner, zai(西 xī)west,
western, ji(二 èr)two,different, kei(京 jīng)the capital of
a country,ten million(an ancient numerals).

105.

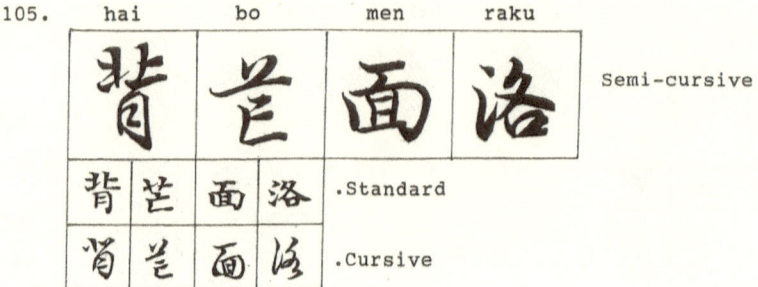

Rakuyo(洛陽 luò yang) in the east is located behind Mt.Bo(邙山 mang shan) and faces Rakusui(洛水 luò shui).
hai(背 bèi)the back of the body,the back of an object, bo(芒 mang) Mt.Bo, men(面 miàn)face,surface,top,side, raku(洛 lùo)a river in Shanxi Province or Henan Province.

106.

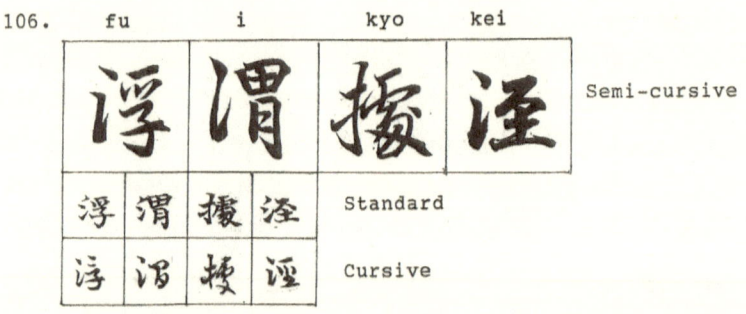

Choan(長安 chang an) in the west is along the Isui(渭水 wèi shui) and Keisui(涇水 jīng shui or 涇河 jin ghe)river. The Isui and the Keisui meet and flow through the Yellow River( Koga 黃河 huang ghe).

107.

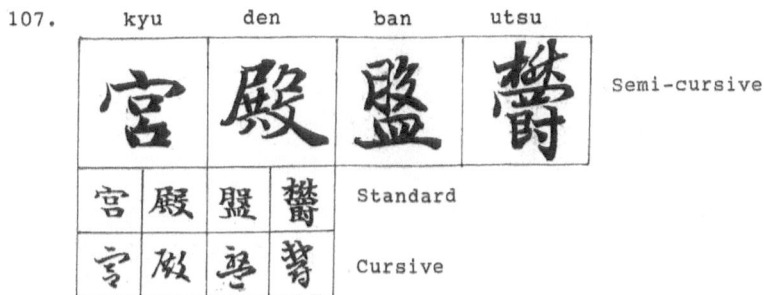

The imperial palaces were built like a coil and ranged.
It was luxuriant view. kyu(宮 gōng)imperial palace,a surname,
womb, den(殿 diàn)hall,palace,temple, ban(鏧 pán)an ancient,
washbaisn,dish,twist,carry,transport,plate,utsu(欝 yù)luxuriant.


108.

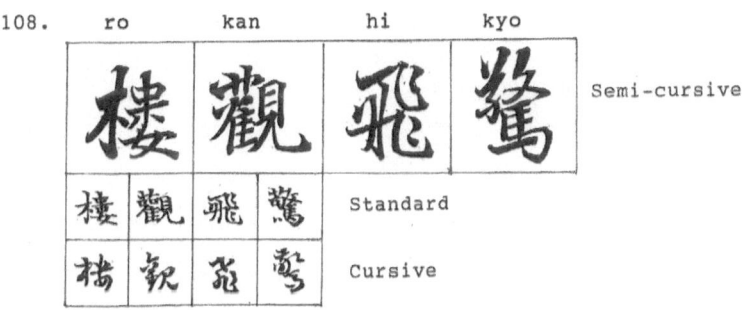

The towers were very high. They looked like flying birds.
People were surprised to see the towers.
ro(樓 lóu)tower,a storied building,floor,a surname, kan(觀 guān)
Taoist temple,look at,watch,view, hi(飛 fēi)fly,flutter in the air,
hover, kyo(驚 jīng)be frightened,surprise,shy,stampede.

109.

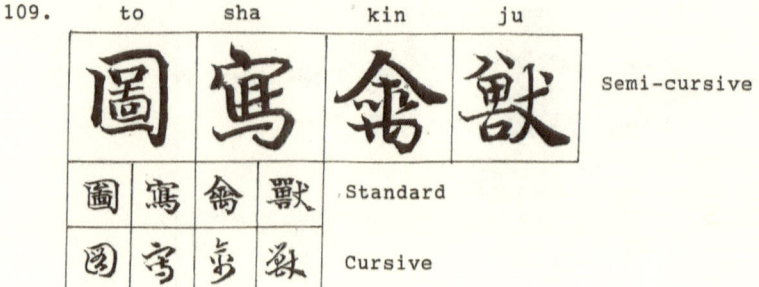

Birds and animals were depicted on the wall of the palace.
to(圖 tú)picture,drawing,chart,map,plan,intention, sha(寫 xiě)
kin(禽 qín)birds, ju(獸 shòu)beast,animal.

110.

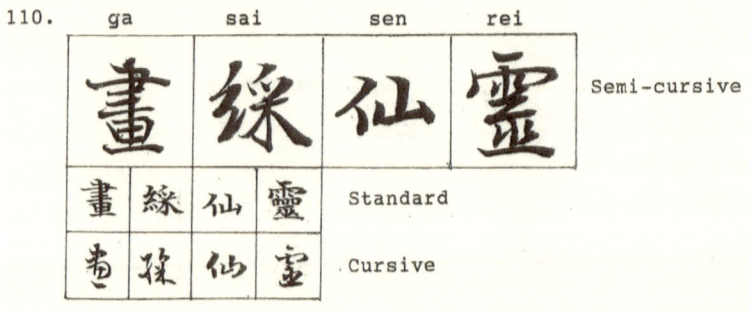

And also we could see hermits and fairies painted with bright colors there.
ga(畫 huà)painting, sai(綵 cǎi)color,cheer,variety,brilliance,
sen(仙 xiān)immortal,celestial, rei(靈 líng)quick,clever,sharp,
spirit,effective.

111.

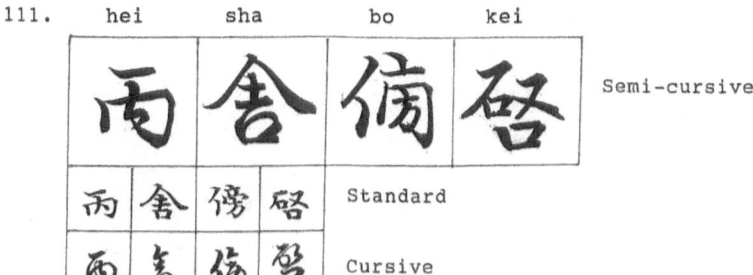

The sides of houses in the palace were opened to be able to go in and out.  hei(丙 bǐng)third,the third of ten heavenly,stems, sha(舍 shè)house,hut,my place,shed, bo(傍 páng)side,lateral radical of Chinese character, kei(啓 qǐ)open,start,initiate,enlighten,state.

112.

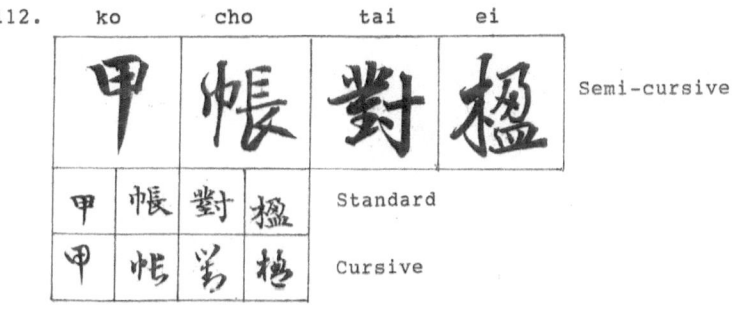

The contrast between curtains and pillars of the imperial palace was very impressive.  ko(甲 jiǎ)shell,first rate,class A,the first of the ten Heavenly stems, cho(帳 zhàng)curtain,account,bill,debt, canopy,account book, tai(對 duì)answer,treat,counter,face to face, oppose,set,, ei(楹 yíng)a pillar.

113.  shi    en    setsu    seki

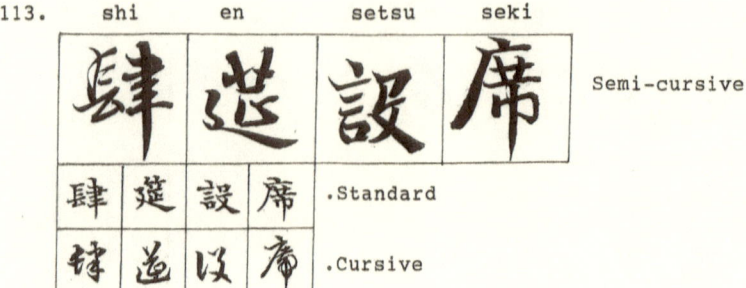

The emperor organized a gathering after placing cushions everywhere. si(肆 sì)wanton,four used for the numerals on cheques,en(筵 yán) formerly,a bamboo mat spread on the floor for people to sit,feast, setsu(設 shè)set up,establish,found,work out,given, seki(席 xí) seat,place,feast banquet,dinner,a surname.


114.  ko    shitsu    sui    sho

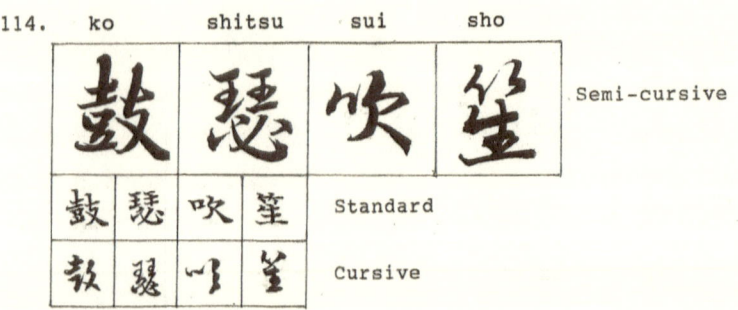

Then a musician performed the harp and the another played the flute for the party.  ko(鼓 gǔ)drum,a thing like drum,beat,strike,rouse, shitsu(瑟 sè)a twenty-five-stringed or sixteen stringed plucked musical instrument,somewhat similar to the zither, sui( 吹chūi) blow,puff,play wind instruments, sho(笙 shēng)a reed pipe wind instrument.

115.     sho      kai      no      hei

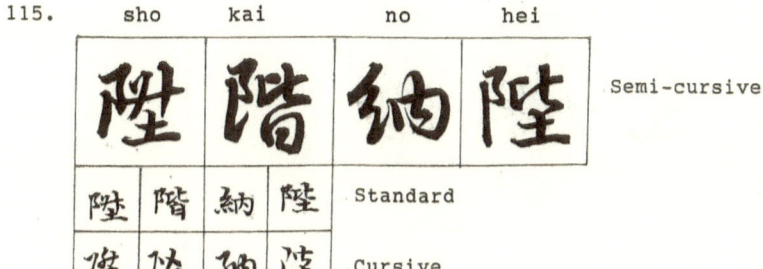

Many palace employees(deputies) had to go up the stairs and to enter the palace.  sho(升 shēng)litre,rise,go up,ascend, kai(階 jiē)steps,stairs,rank, no(納 nà)accept,admit,enjoy,pay,offer, hei(陛 bì)a flight of steps leading to a palace hall.


116.     ben      ten      gi      sei

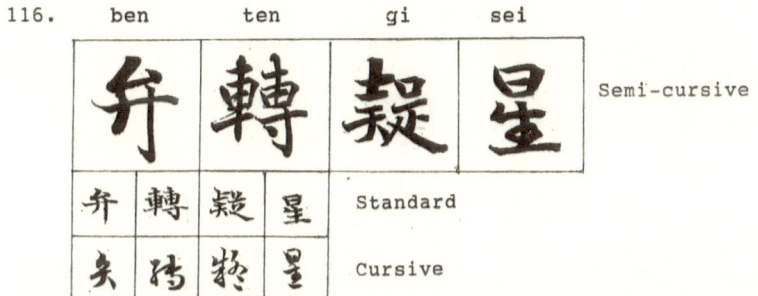

When they moved to the party site,their crowns named Ben(弁 bian) were decorated with beads like shiny stars.
ben(弁 biàn)a man's cap used in ancient times, ten(轉 zhuǎn)turn, shift,change,pass on,transfer, gi(疑 yí)doubt,suspect,uncertain, sei(星 xīng)star,heavenly body,bit.

117.

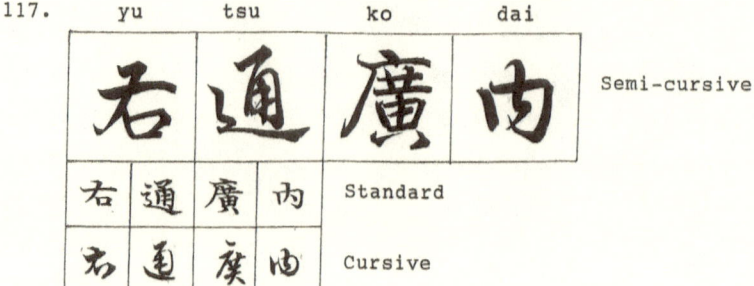

There were Kodai(廣内殿 guǎn nèi diàn) palaces in the east(right), yu(右 yòu)the right side,the right,west,tsu(通 tōng)a complete course, ko(廣 guǎng)wide,broad,vast,numerous, dai(内 nèi)inside, inner part,one's wife or her relatives.

118.

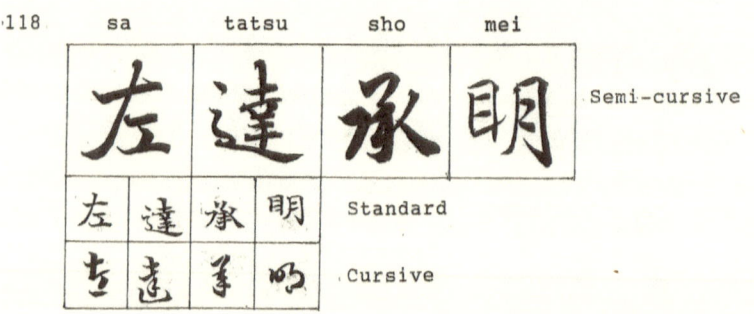

and Shomeiden(承明殿 chéng míng diàn) in the west(left). sa(左 zuǒ)the left,the left side,east,queer,incorrect, tatsu(達 dá) extend,reach,understand throughly,express, sho(承 chéng)bear,hold, mei(明 míng)bright,brilliant,clear,open,sharp-eyed,honest.

119.

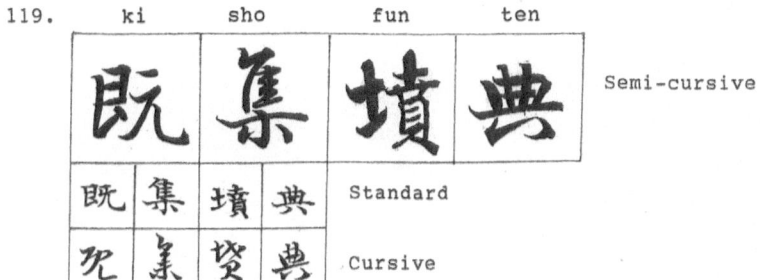

ki sho fun ten — Semi-cursive / Standard / Cursive

The library in the palace collected many books like the Funten(墳典
五典 fén diǎn)=Sanfungoten          san fen wu dian).
Sanpun(三墳 sān fén)1.Futsugi(伏犧 fu xi)2.Shinno(神農 shen nong)
3.Koteinosho(黄帝之畫 huang di zhi shū).
Goten(五典 wǔ diǎn)1.Shoko(少昊 shao hao)2.Sengyoku(顓頊 zhun xu)
3.Koshin(高辛 gao xin)4.To(唐 tang)5.Gu(虞 yu).
Above listed terms are the books of ancient China.

120.

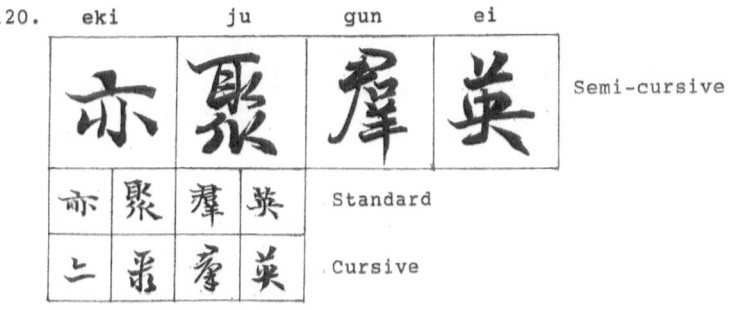

eki ju gun ei — Semi-cursive / Standard / Cursive

Wise people gathered, read and discussed these books with each
other. eki(亦 yì)also,too, ju(聚 jù)gather,assemble,get together,
gun(羣 gún)crowed,group,flock,herd, ei(英 yīng)wise,petal,hero,
England,a surname,outstanding person.

121.　　to　　ko　　sho　　rei

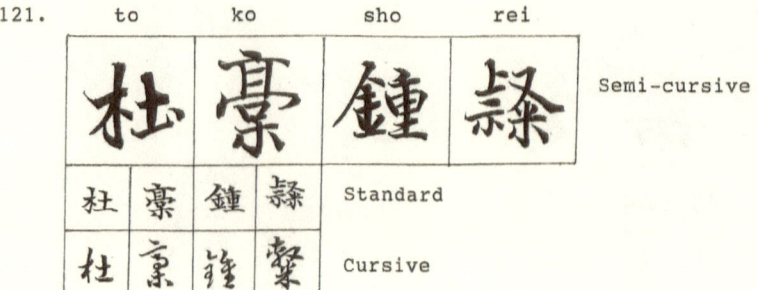

To(杜 dù=Toso 杜操 du cāo) made a brush with straws for the first time. to(杜 du)birch-leaf pear, surname, ko(槀 gǎo)straw,sketch, stalk of grain,a rough draft, sho(鍾 zhōng)bell,clock,time as measured in hours and minutes.
He was good at the clerical style(reisho 隸書 lì shū).
鍾繇(隸) shorei(zhōng lì).

122.　　shitsu　　sho　　heki　　kei

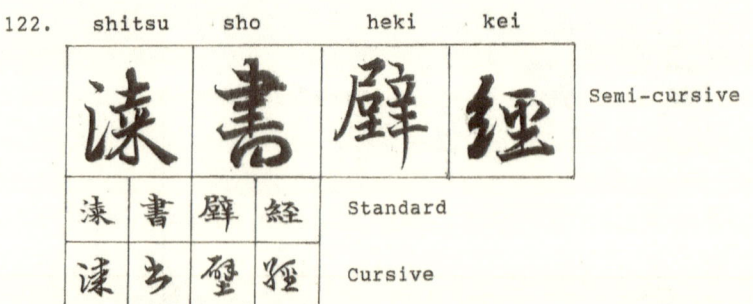

The library of the palace had a good collection of books written with lacquer and sutras on the shelves on the walls.
shitsu(溱 qī)lacquer,paint,coat with lacquer,a surname, sho(書 shu) write,style of calligraphy,book,letter,document, heki(壁 bì)wall, rampart, kei(經 jīng)sutra,longitude.

123.

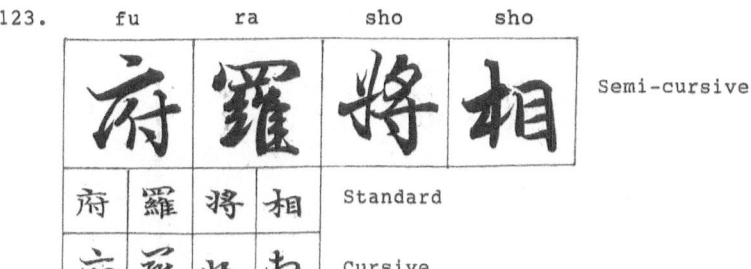

Shoso(将相 jiāng xiāng) in the government, there was a general and ministers who had a star, two to five stars.
fu(府 fǔ)seat of government,government,mansion,official residence, ra(羅 lí)thin silk,net, sho(将 jiāng)support,take,bring,take care of one's health,handle a matter, sho(相 xiāng)each other,mutually, one another,a surname.
Shoso(将相 jiāng xiāng)1.Shogun 将軍 2.Saisho 宰相 zai xiang
　　　　　　　　　　　　　 jiāng jun

124.

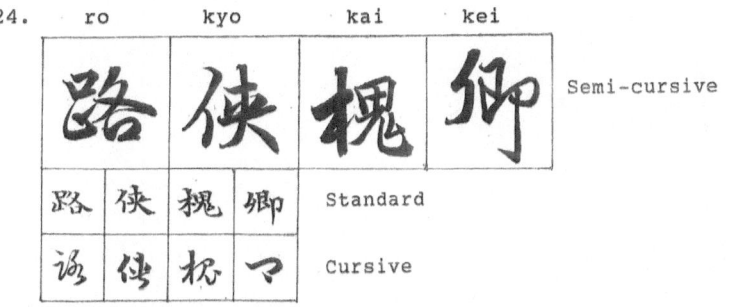

Kaikei(槐卿 huái qīng) like the government guards stood in line on the street, and judged the common people's request.
ro(路 lu)road,path,way,journey,distance,line,logic,grade,class, a surname, kyo(侠 xiá)having a strong sense of justice and ready to help the weak, kai(槐 huái)Chinese scholartree, kei(卿 qīng) a minister or a high official in ancient times.

125.

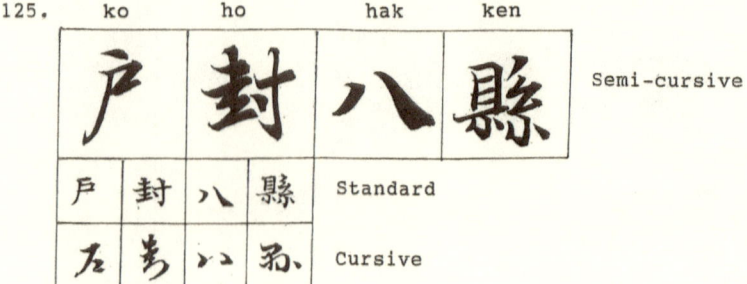

If a high official had distinguished services, a house and 8 block lots were given to him. ko(戶 hù)door,household,family status, a house,bank account, ho(封 fēng)seal,wrapper, hatsu(八 bā)eight, ken(縣 xiàn)county.

126.

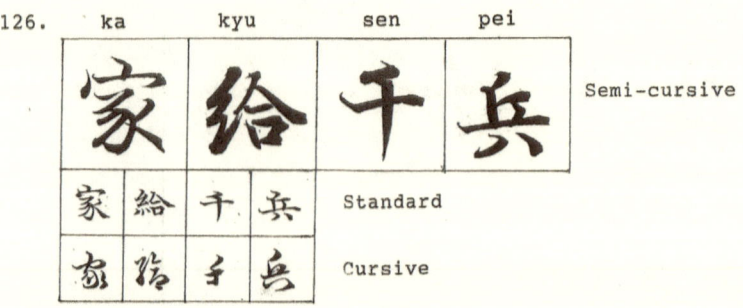

One thousand soldiers were offered to a creditable officials. ka(家 jiā)family,household,home,domestic,school,a specialist in a certain field, kyu(給 gěi)give,grant,let,make, sen(千 qiān)thousand, a surname,a great amount of, pei(兵 bīng)weapon,arms,soldier,pawn, troop,military.

127.    ko      kan     bai     ren

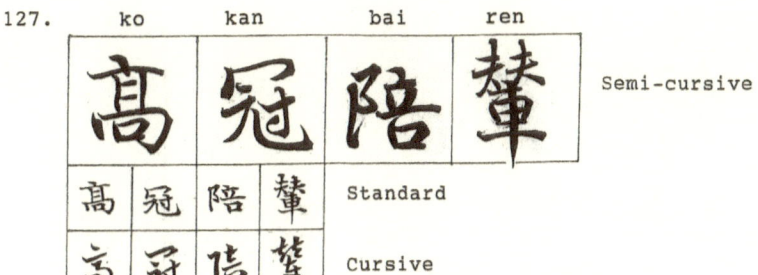

Semi-cursive
Standard
Cursive

A high-ranking official was able to get in the emperor's carriage. ko(高 gāo)high,tall,loud,expensive,a surname, kan(冠 gūan)hat, crown,crest,comb, bai(陪 péi)accompany,keep one company, ren(輦 niǎn)imperial carriage,a man-drawn carriage used in ancient times.


128.    ku      koku    shin    ei

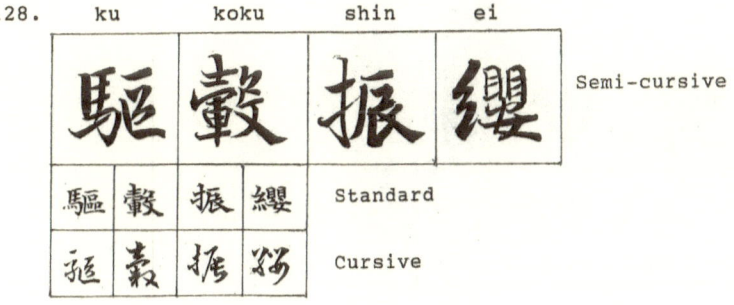

Semi-cursive
Standard
Cursive

When the wheels started to move, the sashes of the Emperor's crown shaked like a horse gallop.  ku(驅 qu)drive a horse or a car, run quickly, koku(轂 gǔ)hub, shin(振 zhèn)shake,flap, ei(纓 ying) ribbon,tassel.

129.

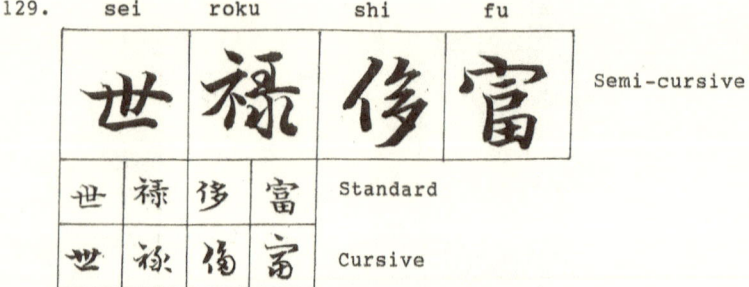

The officials in feudal China who inherited their ancestors' properties were wasteful and rich.
sei(世 shì)life time,life,generation,age,the world, roku(禄 lù) official's in feudal China, shi(侈 chǐ)wasteful, fu(富 fù)wealthy,

130.

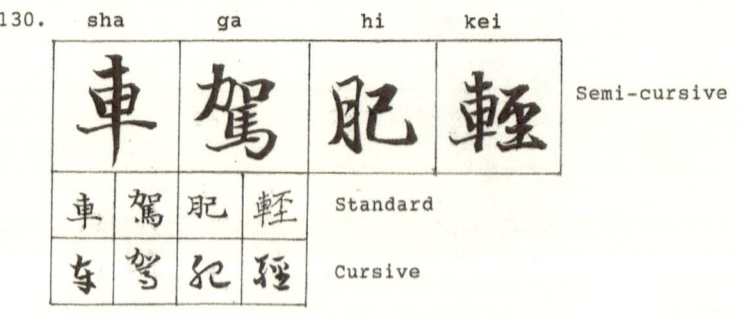

They had fat horse carriages and wore light leather jackets. (This means very rich.)  sha(車 chē)vehicle,a wheeled instrument, machine,turn,a surname, ga(駕 jià)hardness,drive a vehicle,pilot a plane,sail a boat,the Emperor, hi(肥 féi)fat,rich,fertilize, (fu)clothes,wear,put on,serve, kei(軽 qīng)light,small in number, not important,soft,gentle,relaxing.

131. saku　ko　mo　jitsu

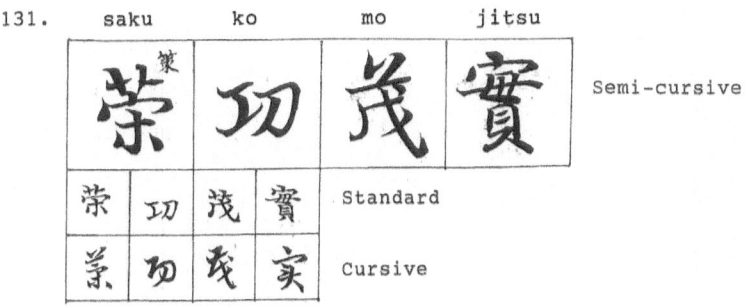

Semi-cursive / Standard / Cursive

An official's remarkable service was recorded.
saku(策 cè)bamboo,wooden slips used for writing on in ancient China,
ko(功 gōng)result,effect,skill,meritorious service or deed,merit,
mo( 茂 mào)rich and splendid,profuse,luxuriant, jitsu(實 shí)solid,
true,real,fact,fruit,seed,actual.


132. roku　hi　koku　mei

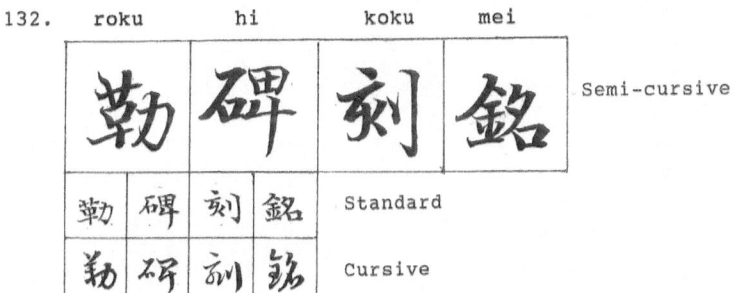

Semi-cursive / Standard / Cursive

If the official's distinguished service was substantial, his name
was engraved on the stone monument and would live forever.
roku(勒 lè)engrave,carve,force,coerce, hi(碑 bēi)stele,an upright
stone tablet, koku(刻 kè)carve,engrave,cut,unkind,moment, mei(銘
míng)inscription,engrave.

133.

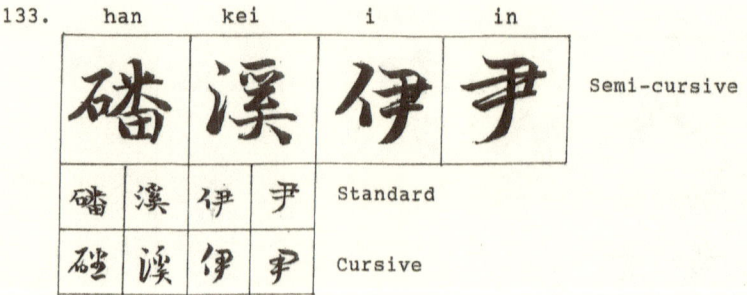

Hankei(磻溪 pán xī) is the name of a place(small stream), and it became of a person's name later. The place that Taikobo(太公望 tai gong wang) used to go fishing. Hankei is the name of small stream,brook, i(伊 yi)he,she,a surname,Italy, in(尹 yǐn)ancient official title,a surname.

134.

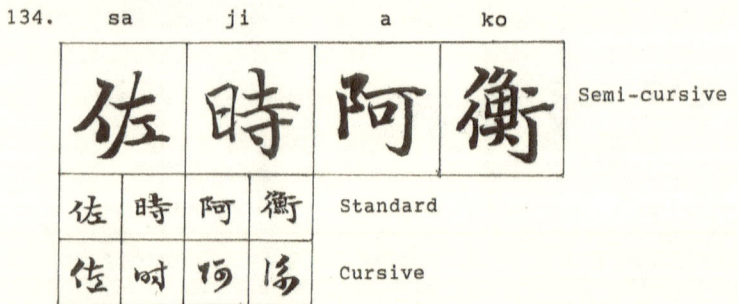

sa 佐 zuǒ

Hankei and Iin(伊尹 yi yin) helped the Emperor of the period and saved the nation. Ako(阿衡 ā hēng) is the name of a position or Emperor's request. sa(佐 help,assist, ji(時 shí)times,a surname, now and then,hour,time of day,a long period of time,present, a(阿 ā)a prefix, ko(衡 héng)weigh,measure,judge,weighing apparatus.

135.

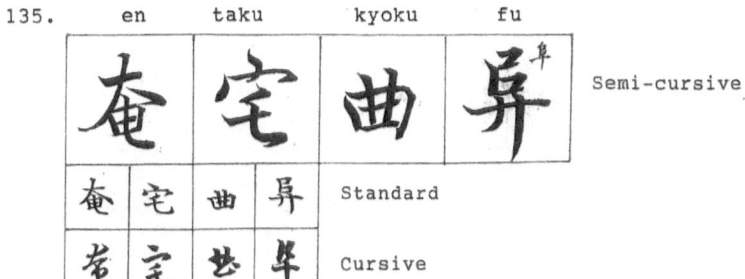

Semi-cursive / Standard / Cursive

Tan(shukotan 周公旦 zhōu gōng dàn) built a big palace spread all over Kyokufu(曲阜 qū fù). en(奄 yǎn)big cover,include,suddenly, taku(宅 zhái)residence,house, kyoku(曲 qū)song,tune,a type of verse for singing, fu(阜 fù)mound.

136.

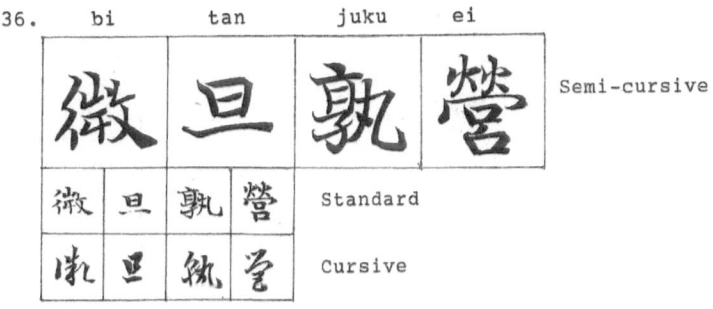

Semi-cursive / Standard / Cursive

If Tan was not here, nobody could build the palace like this. (cira 1020 B.C.) The Emperor Buo(武王 wǔ wáng) admired Tan's conduct. bi(微 wēi)minute,tiny,slight,profound, tan(旦 dàn)dawn, daybreak,day, juku(孰 shú)who,which,what, ei(營 yíng)camp,operate, barracks.

137.

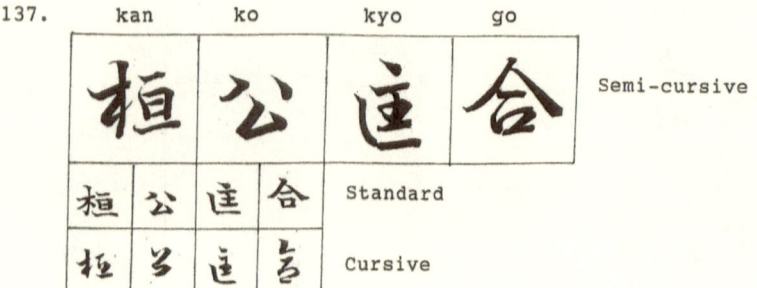

Kanko (桓公 huán gōng) gathered his followers and put down (surppressed) a revolt against the ruler.
kan(桓 huán)a surname, ko(公 gōng)public,duke,husband's father, kyo(匡 kuāng)correct,save,assist,rectify,a surname, go(合 hé)join, combine,close,shut,suit,be equal to,add up.
  kyo 匡 kuāng

138.

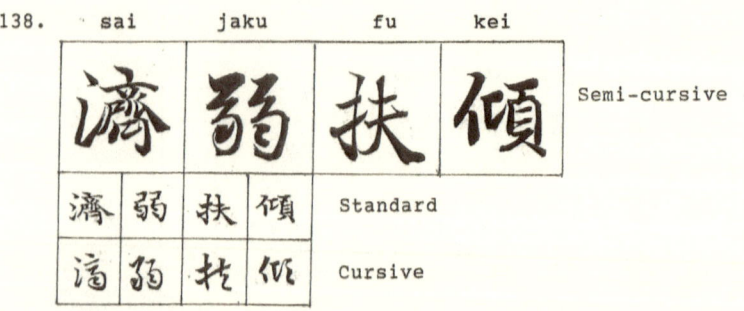

sai 濟, 济 jì
He saved the weak people or countries and the followers' prejudice.
sai(濟 jì)aid,help,relieve,save,benefit, jaku(弱 ruō)weak,feeble,young, fu(扶 fú)support with the hand,help,support, kei(傾 qīng).

139.

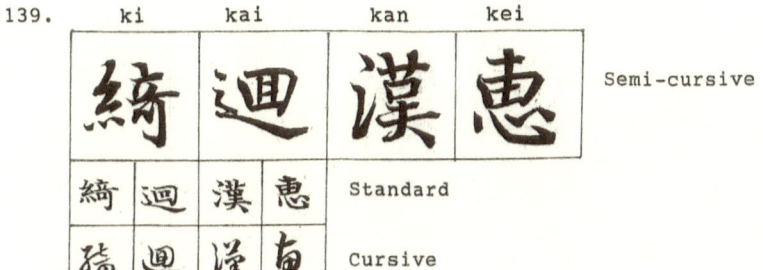

Kiriki(綺里季 qǐ lǐ jì) considered Kankei(漢恵 hàn huì) and thought his future deeply. ki(綺 qi)damask,figured woven silk, beautiful, kai(迴 huí)circle,return,go back,time, kan(漢 hàn) Chinese language,the Han Dynasty 206B.C. - 220A.D.,the Milky Way, kei(恵 huì)favour,kindness,benefit,a surname.

140.

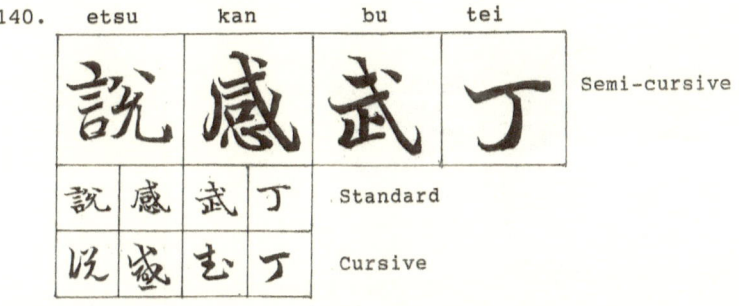

Etsu(Fusetsu 傅說 fù shuō) took in Butei(武丁 wǔ dīng)'s situation and helped Bu's new position.
etsu(說 shuō)speak,talk,say,explain,theory,teachings,indicate, kan(感 gǎn)feel,sense,move,touch,be obliged, bu(武 wǔ)military, swordplay,fierce,a surname, tei(丁 dīng)small cubes of meat or vegetables,man,members of a family,a surname,a person engaged in a certain occupation,a surname.

141. shun gai mitsu futsu

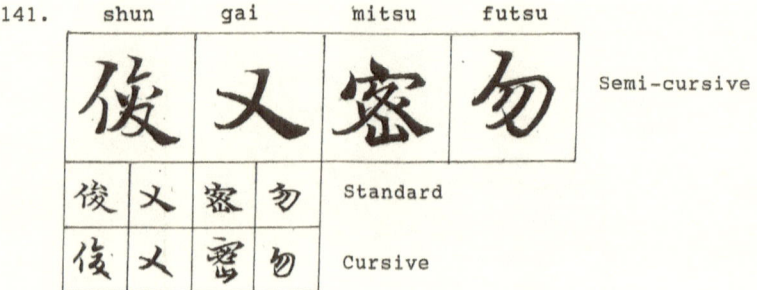

Semi-cursive

Standard

Cursive

The Emperor was familiar with his potential retainers(followers) and, shun(俊 jùn)outstanding talent,handsome,pretty,talented, gai(乂 yì)put in order,store,warn,wise man,cut, mitsu(密 mì)dense, butsu(勿 wù)do not,never,flag.
shun 俊, 儁, 雋 jùn

142. ta shi shoku nei

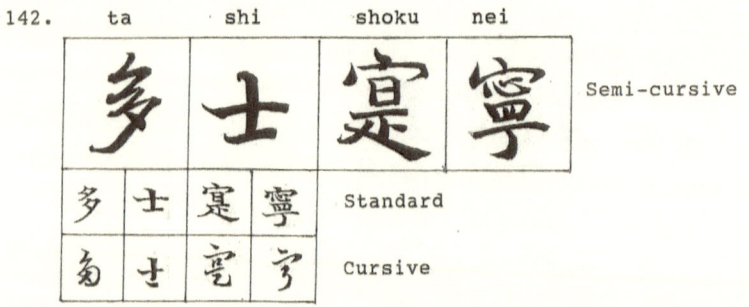

Semi-cursive

Standard

Cursive

Many of them gathered at the court. After this, the political state was very stable. ta(多 duō)many,much,more,too much, shi(士 shì)bachelor in ancient China,scholar,soldier,armyman, the common people, shoku(寔 shí)very,this,truth,nothing but, nei(寧 níng)peaceful,tranquil,another name for Nanjing.

143.

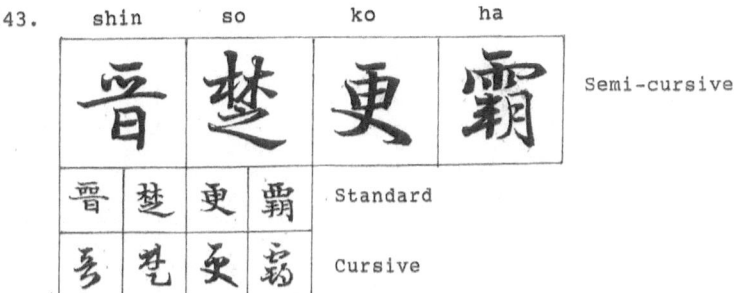

The countries of Shin(晋 jìn) and So(楚 chǔ) conquered other small countries one after another. shin(晋 jìn)enter,advance,a state in the Zhou Dynasty, so(楚 chǔ)clear,neat,suffering,one of the warring states into which China was divided during the Eastern Zhou period 770 - 256 B.C.,a surname, ko(更 gēng)replace,change,experience, more,even more,further, ha(霸 bà)leader of feudal lords,dominate, bully,despot.

144.

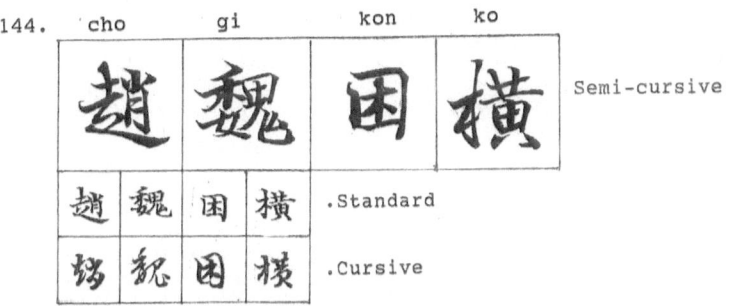

Rikkoku(六国 liu guo) 6 countries 1.So(楚 chǔ) 2.En(燕 yān) 3.Sei(齊 qí) 4.kan(韓 hán) 5.Gi(儀 yí) 6.Cho(趙 zhào).

Cho(趙 zhào) and Gi(魏 wei) were tormented with the trick of Cho(張 zhang) and Gi(儀 yi) from Shin(秦 qin). cho(趙 zhào)a surname, one of the warring states into which China was divided during the Eastern Zhou period, gi(魏 wèi)a surname,one of warring states into which China was divided during the Eastern Zhou period 770 - 256 B.C., kon(囲 kùn)be stranded,be hard pressed,tired,surround, ko(横 héng)horizontal,sideway,from east to west,from west to east, crosswise.

145.

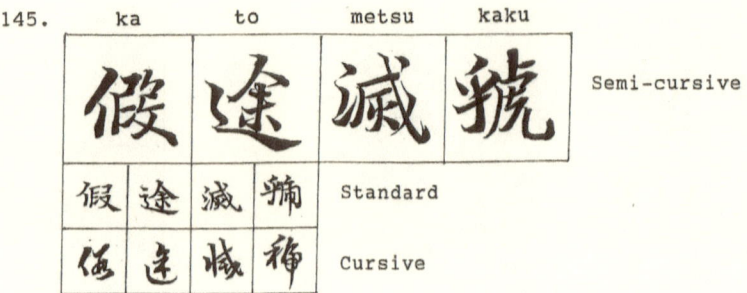

Kenko(獻公 xian gōng) went through the roads of Gu(虞 yú) country and destroyed Kaku(虢 guo), when returning, Kenko also ruined Gu(虞 yú). ka(假 jiǎ)false,fake,sham,phoney,if,artificial,borrow, to(途 tu)way,road,route, metsu(滅 miè)go out,turn off,submerge, destroy, kaku(虢 guó)the name of country,(Zhou Dynasty).

Kaku 虢, 虢 guó

146.

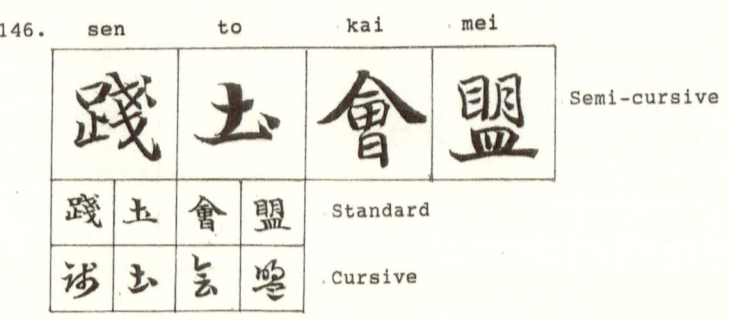

Bunko(文公 wén gōng) gathered the followers together at Sento(踐土 jian tu: place name) and promised to plead, it means they shared to drink their blood of one another. (kaimei 會盟 huì méng). sen(踐 jian)trample,act on,carry out, to(土 tu)soil, earth,land,ground,local,native,homemade, kai(會 hui)get together, meet,see,gathering, mei(盟 meng)alliance,league.

147.      ka      jun      yaku      ho

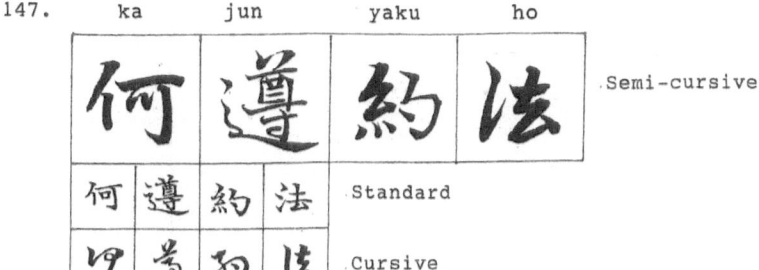

Semi-cursive
Standard
Cursive

Ka(shoka 蕭何 xiao hé) obeyed and surmarized the law. After this, law and order restored in the era. ka(何 he)what,which,how,why, a surname, jun(遵 zūn)obey,observe,follow, yaku(約 yuē)arrange, make an appointment,invite in advance,frugal, ho(法 fǎ)law,method, standard,model,follow,mode.

148.      kan      hei      han      kei

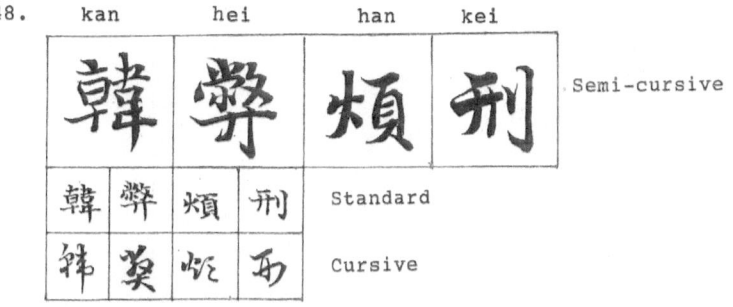

Semi-cursive
Standard
Cursive

Kan(kanpishi 韓非子 hán fēi zǐ) enforced strict laws. the nation suffered from the law. And Kan led Shin( 秦 qín) nation's fall. kan( 韓 han)a surname,The Republic of Korea, hei( 弊 bì)abuse,fraud, harm,disadvantage, han( 煩 fan)be annoyed,bother,be tired of, kei( 刑 xíng)punishment,torture.

149.

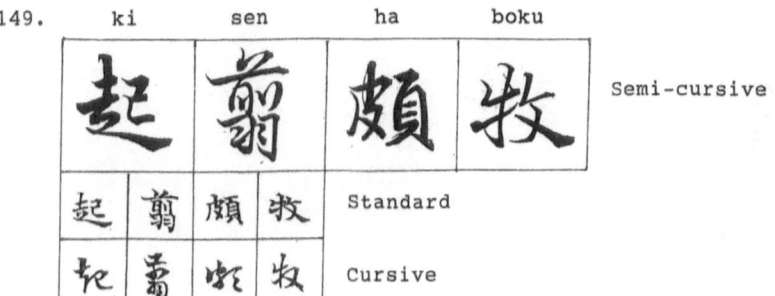

Four of generals were Ki(Hakki 伯起 bo qǐ), Sen(Osen 王翦 wang jiǎn) Ha(Renpa 廉頗 lian pō) and Boku(Riboku 李牧 li mù)). ki(起 qi) get up,rise,stand up,set up,start,begin, sen(翦 jian)a surname, ha(頗 pō)quite,rather,considerably, boku(牧 mù)tend sheep,cattle.

150.

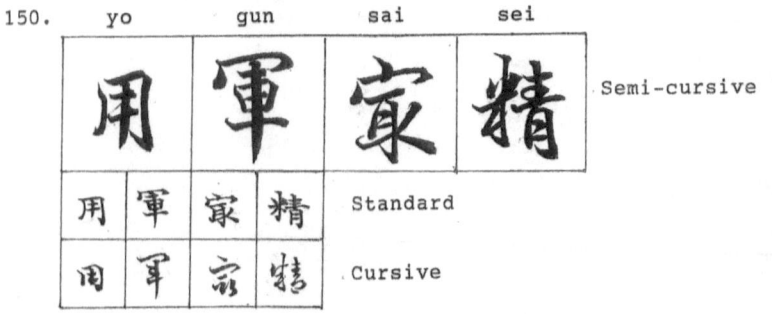

They knew how to use the troops very well.
yo(用 yòng)use,employ,apply,with,therefore,need,outlay, gun(軍 jūn)army,troops, sai(寂 zùi)most,nearest a place,..est, sei(精 jìng)refind,choice,semen,picked,perfect,excellent,smart,skilled.

151.    sen     i      sa     baku

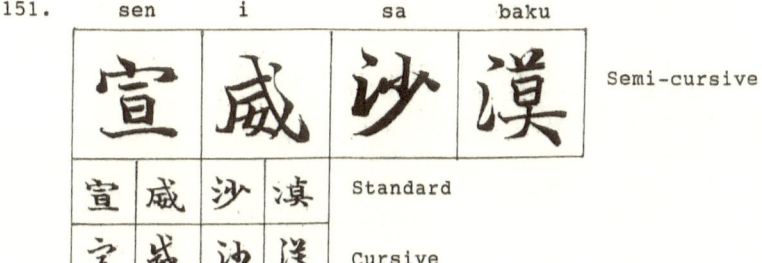

Semi-cursive
Standard
Cursive

i(威 wēi :noted general) became widely known even Ebisu(狄 di) desert. sen(宣 xuān)declare,proclaim,announce,drain,a surname, i(威 wēi)impressive,strength,might,power,by force, sa(沙 shā)sand, grit,powdery,a surname, baku(漠 mò)desert,indifferent,unconcerned.


152.    chi     yo     tan    sei

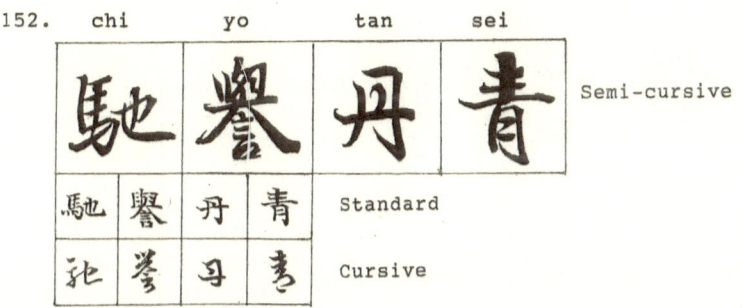

Semi-cursive
Standard
Cursive

According to his honor, his portraits were painted with red and blue. And as a great general he would live forever in their nation's descendants' memory. chi(馳 chí)spread,gallop,speed of horses,vehicles, yo(譽 yù)reputation,fame,eulogize, tan(丹 dān) red, sei(青 qīng)blue,green,green grass,young crops,young people.

153. kyu    shu    u    seki

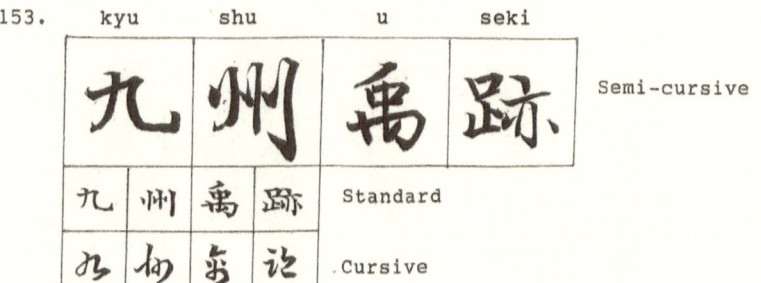

Semi-cursive / Standard / Cursive

Kyushu(九州 jǐu zhōu)nine states were 1.ki(冀 jì) 2.kon(袞 gǔn) 3.sei(青 qīng) 4.jo(徐 xú) 5.yo(揚 yáng) 6.kei(荊 jīng) 7.yo(豫 yù) 8.ryo(梁 liáng) and 9.yo(雁 yan). King U(禹 yǔ) reclaimed land from the nine states and made agricultural states. Useki(禹跡 yǔ jì) means U 禹's country. kyu(九 jiu)ninen,many, numerous, shu(州 zhou)prefecture,an administrative division in former times, u(禹 yu)the reputed founder of the Xia Dynasty C. 21st - 16th century B.C., a surname, seki(跡 jī)mark,trace, remain,ruins,(ji)vestige,indication,an outward sign.

154. haku    gun    shin    hei

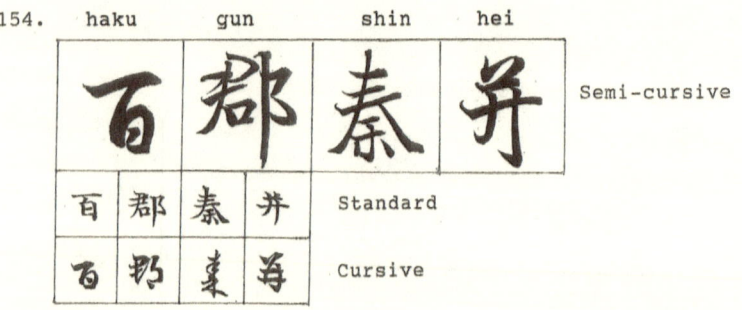

Semi-cursive / Standard / Cursive

Shinshiko(秦始皇 qín shǐ huáng 259 B.C. - 210 B.C.) linked countries altogether and made one hundred states (another theory: 36 states). haku(百 bǎi)hundred,numerous,all kinds of, gun(郡 jùn)prefecture, shin(秦 qín)one of the warring states into which China was divided during the Eastern Zhou period 770 B.C. - 256 B.C., hei(并 bìng)combine,merge,incorporate,equally.

155.  gaku   so   ko   tai

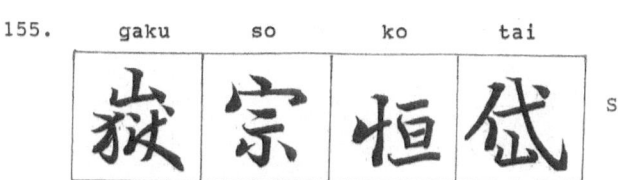

Semi-cursive
Standard
Cursive

Gaku(嶽 yuè) called five mountains(Gogaku 五嶽 wu yue)
1.Taizan(秦山 qin shan = togaku 東岳 dōng yuè) 2.Kazan(華山 hua shān = seigaku 西岳 xi yue) 3.Suzan(崇山 song shan = chugaku 中岳 zhōng yuè) 4.Kozan(衡山 héng shān = nangaku 南岳 nán yuè) and 5.Kozan(恒山 hēng shān = hokugaku 北岳 běi yuè).
Mt.Ko was located in Taishu(岱州 dai zhōu) state and the mountain was the head rank among the five mountains. gaku(嶽yuè)high mountain,wife's parent(ex. gakufu岳父 yuèfu), so(宗 zōng)sect, ancestor,clan,model,great master,aim,purpose,a surname, ko(恒 kēng)permanent,lasting,(heng)usual,common,perseverance, tai(岱 dài)another name for Taizan(秦山 taishan) = Taigaku秦岳 dai yuè.

156.  zen   shu   un   tei

Semi-cursive
Standard
Cursive

The best place for the Zen Buddhism training was Mt.Untei(云亭山 yun ting shan).   zen(禅 chán)Buddhism,deep meditation,Buddhist, contemplation, shu(主 zhǔ)host,owner,master,main,manage,direct, indicate,signify, un(云 yún)say,cloud,short for(unnan云南 Yúnnan), tei(亭 tíng)pavilion in a park,a road for people to rest.

157. gan mon shi sai

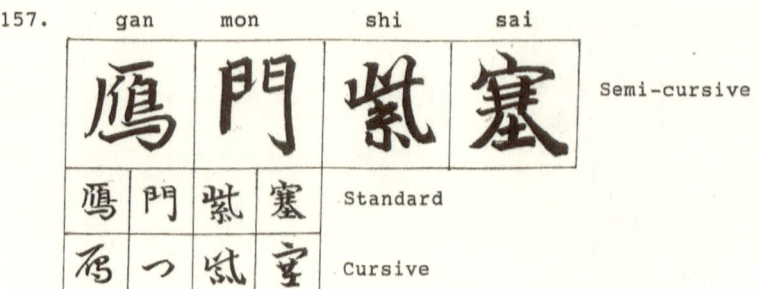

Semi-cursive / Standard / Cursive

Wild goose gate(ganmon鴈門 yàn mén) and the Great Wall of China (Banrinochojo万里之長城 wan lǐ zhī cháng chéng). Mt.Tai(taizan 岱山 dai shan) was a high mountain. Only wild geese were able to fly over one spot of mountain. So, people called the wild goose gate for the mountain. The Great Wall of China was named Shisai(紫塞 zǐ sāi), because the color of the Wall was purple soil. gan(鴈 yàn)wild goose, mon(門 men)gate,door,entrance,way to do, knack,family, shi(紫 zǐ)purple,violet, sai(塞 sāi)fill in,stuff, stopper,(sai)a place of strategic importance.

158. kei den seki jo

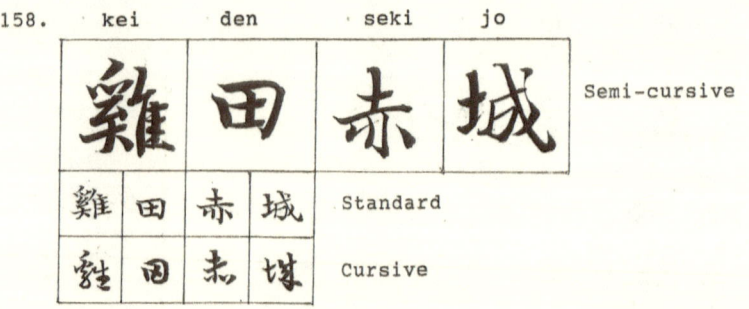

Semi-cursive / Standard / Cursive

Keiden(雞田 jī tian: station name) was located in Sekijo(赤城 chì chéng): the ruin of barrier during the Shu(周 zhou) Dynasty 1020 B.C. - 227 B.C., kei(雞 jī)chicken,cock, den(田 tían)field, farmland,cropland,a surname,go hunting, seki(赤 chì)red,loyal, sincere,bare,revolutionary,communist, jo(城 chéng)castle.

159. kon　chi　ketsu　seki

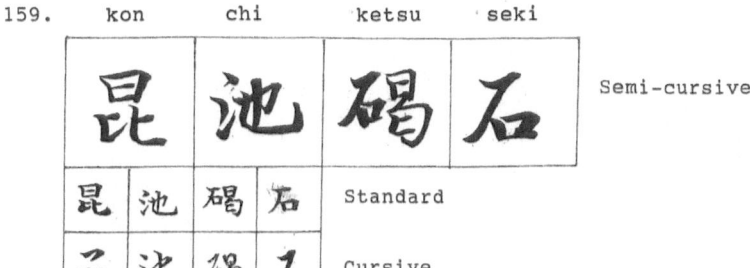

Semi-cursive
Standard
Cursive

Konchi(昆池 kūn chí = konmeichi 昆明池 kun míng chí) and Kessuseki(碣石 zhēn shí : Mt.Kessuseki). kon(昆 kūn)offspring, elder brother, chi(池 chí)pond,pool,stall in a theatre,orchestra, a surname,ketsu(碣 zhēn)a stone monument,a stone pillar, seki(石 shí)stone,rock,stone inscription,a surname.

160. kyo　ya　do　tei

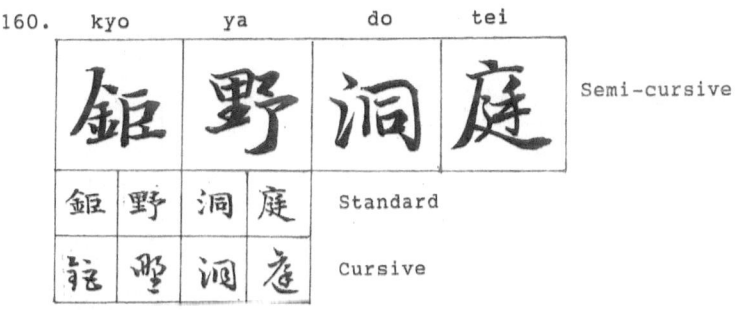

Semi-cursive
Standard
Cursive

Kyoya(鉅野 jù yè : Kyoya wilderness) in Kyorokugun(鉅鹿郡 ju lù jùn: Kyoroku country) and Doteiko(洞庭湖 dòng tíng hú : lake Dotei). kyo(鉅 jù)huge,tremendous,gigantic, ya(野 yè) open county,the open,limit,not in power,rude,rough, do(洞 dòng)

hole,cavity,penetratingly,thoroughly, tei(庭 tíng)front courtyard, law court.

161.    ko      en      men     baku

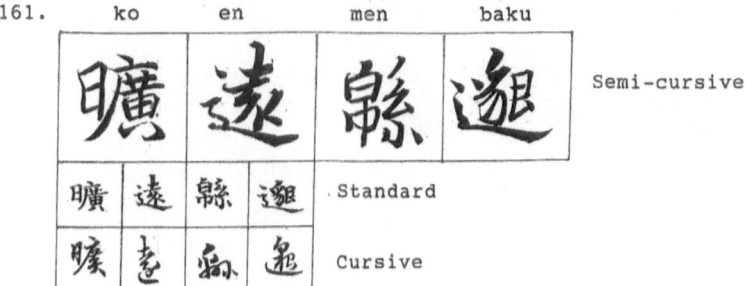

These mountains and streams were extensive and far.
( I saw dim landscape in the distance.) ko(曠 kuàng)vast,spacious,
en(遠 yuǎn)far away,distant in relationship,keep away from,
men(縣 mián)silk floss,continuous,soft, baku(邈 miǎo)faraway,remote.


162    gan     shu      yo     mei

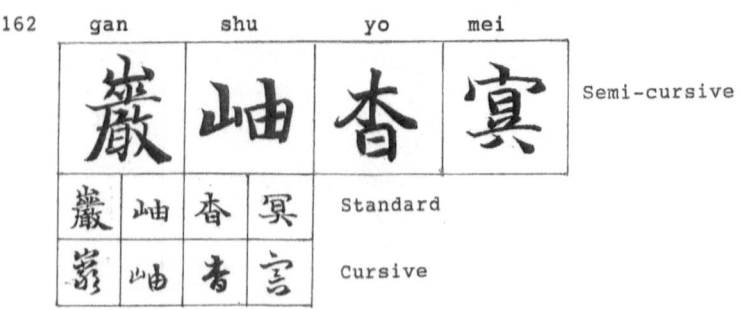

Mountain rocks and caves were endless depth and far.
gan(巖 yán)rocks,cliff,crag, shu(岫 xìu)cave,mountain peak,cavern,
yo(杳 miǎo)dark,far,deep,calm,quiet, mei(冥 míng)dark,deep,dull,
underworld,stupid,obscure.

163.   chi    hon    o    no

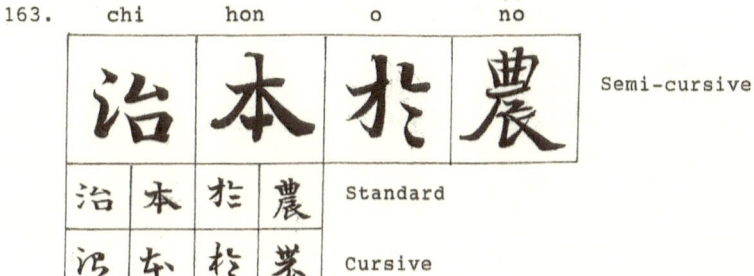

The administration of nation was based on agriculture(no 農 nóng).
chi(治 zhì)rule,administer,manage,order,study,research,control,
hon(本 ben)book,be based on,the root,stem of a plant,foundation,
principle,at first,current, o(於 yú)in,on,at,with regard to,from,
conerning, no(農 nóng)agriculture,farming.


164.   mu    ji    ka    shoku

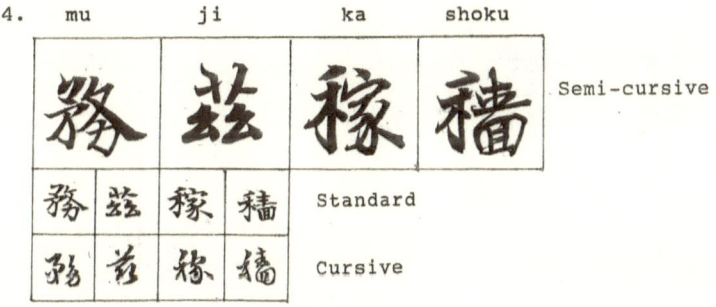

Ka(稼 jià : sowing) and Shoku(穡 sè : sowing and grain harvest)
became prosperous, so ,people worked hard. mu(務 wù)affair,must,
business,be engaged in, ji(茲 zī)this,now,at present,increase,
straw-mat.

165.

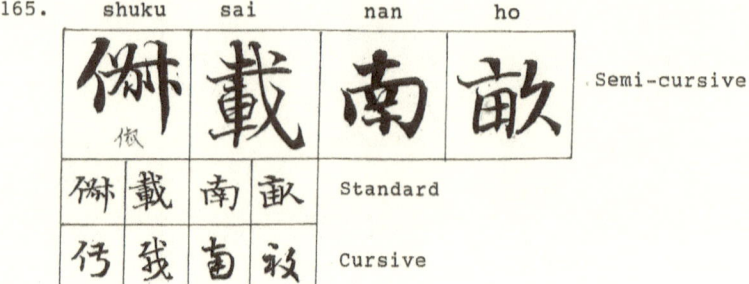

First we sowed cereals in the south field.
shuku(俶 chù)good,first, sai(載 zài)carry,hold,be loaded with,
all over the road, nan(南 nán)south,monarch,a surname, ho(畝 mǔ)
ridge,cultivation area.

166.

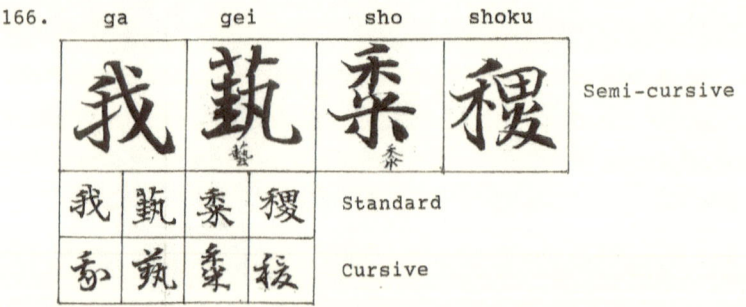

Our duty was to plant millet(kibi 黍 shu) and banyard grass(hie
ji) and work agriculture hard.  ga(我 wǒ)I,me,we,us,self,one,
anyone, gei(藝 yì)skill,art,be in dilemma,limit, sho( 黍 shǔ)
broomcorn millet(Panicum miliaceum), shoku(稷 jì)millet, the god
of grains worshipped by ancient emperors.

167.   zei    juku    ko    shin

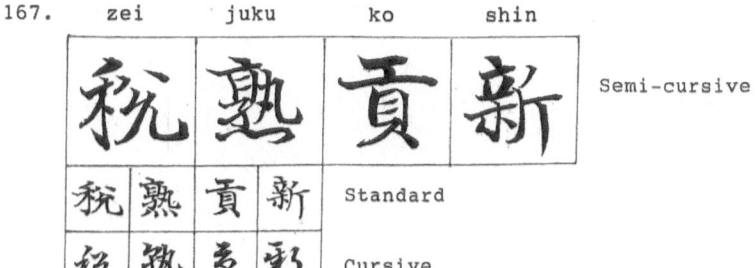

Offering well grown up grains and new kinds of grains as a tax was the duty of farmers. zei(稅 shùi)tax,duty, juku(熟 shóu) boil,mature,mature adult,maturity, ko(貢 gòng)tribute,a surname, shin(新 xìn)new,up to date,unused,recently,newly,fresh.


168.   kan    sho    chutsu   choku

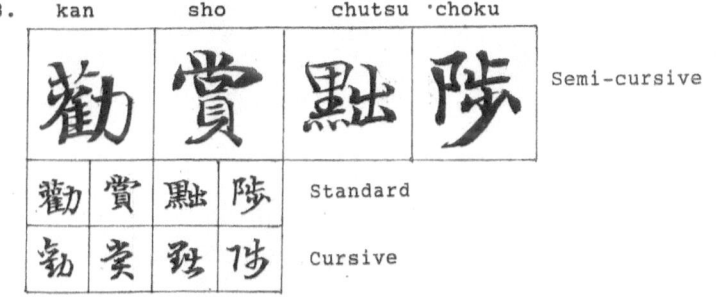

If farmers paid the tax, they were admired and encouraged.
If not, they were crossed off the farmers' list.
kan(勸 quàn)advice,encourage,comfort,try to persuade, sho(賞 shǎng) award,view and admire,recognize,appreciate, chutsu(黜 chū)remove, dismiss, choku(陟 zhì)promote,climb,scale,ascend.

169.  mo   ka   ton   so

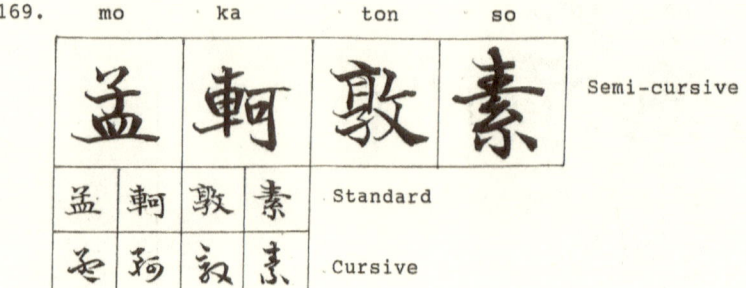

Mo(moshi 孟子 mèng zǐ, ka 軻 kē first name 372 B.C. - 289 B.C.) was a gentle and meek(honest) personality. mo(孟 mèng)head, the first month of a season,the oldest among brothers, and sisters, ka(軻 ke)name,a car has a damaged shaft, ton(敦 dūn)honest,sincere, so(素 sù)white silk,always,plain,simple,native,quiet.


170.  shi   gyo   hei   choku

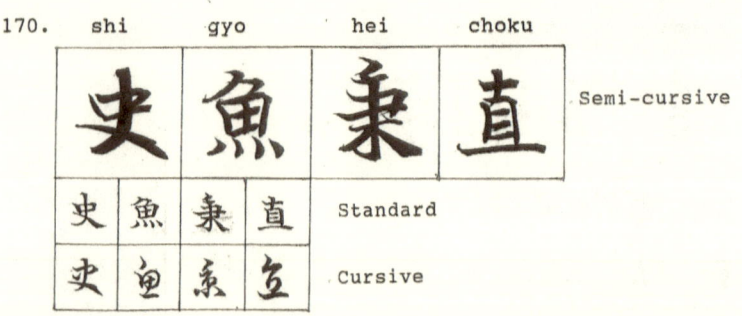

Shigyo(史魚 shǐ yú) was strict and honest(heichoku 秉直 bing zhi) Shigyo = taifu(大夫 dà fū) a position of Ei(衛 wei) country during the Shu(周 zhōu 1020 B.C. - 256 B.C.) Dynasty.
shi(史 shi)history,official historian in ancient China,a surname, gyo(魚 yu)fish, a surname, hei(秉 bǐng)grasp,hold,control,preside over, choku(直 zhí)vertical stroke,directly,just,straight,simply, frank.

171.    sho      ki       chu      yo

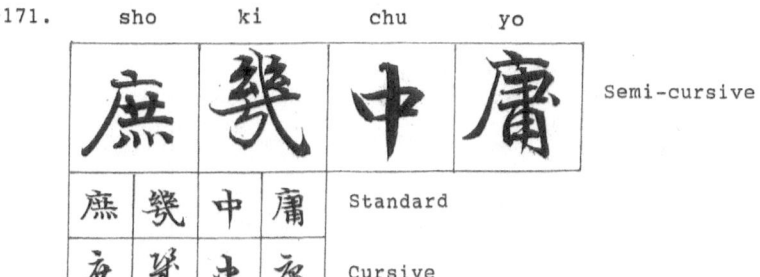

Semi-cursive

Standard

Cursive

We wanted to keep a stable life.
sho(庶 shù)numerous,so that,of,many people,various, ki(幾 jǐ)
how many,a few,some,several,nearly,almost, chu(中 zhōng)center,
among,middle,China,medium, yo(庸 yōng)mediocre,inferior,secondrate.


172.    ro       ken      kin      choku

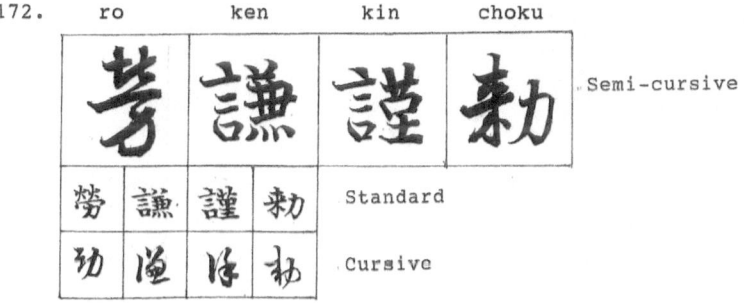

Semi-cursive

Standard

Cursive

Working harder and upright. Be modest(humble) and keep right
conduct.   ro(勞 láo)work,labour,meritorious deed,service,toil,
a surname, ken(謙 qiān)modest,humble,dislike,nice,pleasant, kin(謹
jǐn)careful,cautious,sincerely, choku(勅 chì)edict,imperial order.

173.   rei     in     satsu    ri

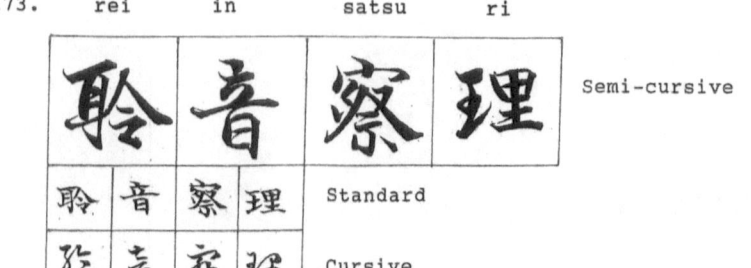

Listen to a person's idea, and recognize the way of life.
rei(聆 líng)listen,hear,follow, in(音 yīn)sound,musical sound,note,
news,syllable, satsu(察 chá)examine,look into,scrutinize, ri(理
lǐ)texture,reason,grain in wood,logic,truth.


174.   kan     bo     ben     shoku

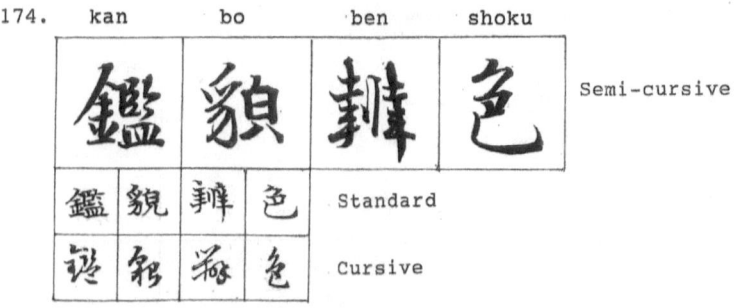

Observe one's countenance and analize the facial expression.
It means we have to pay attention to one's facial expression and
behavior.   kan(鑑 jiàn)mirror,reflect,observe,object lesson,inspect,
bo(貌 mào)looks,appearance,conduct,figure, ben(辡 biàn)crown,fast,
hurry,debate,dispute, shoku(色 sè)colour,look,expression,feminine
charms,sexual desire,description.

175.    i      ketsu    ka     yu

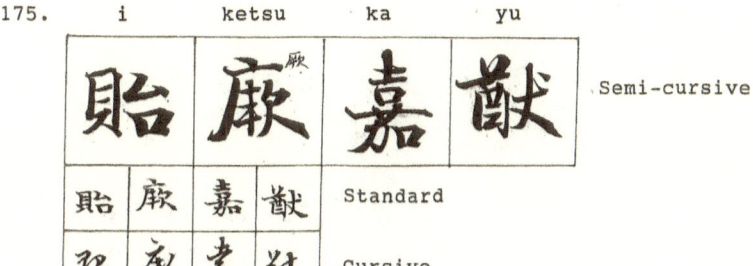

Semi-cursive / Standard / Cursive

A noble man(kunshi 君子 jūn zǐ) left a good project.
i(貽 yí)present,make a gift of, ketsu(厥 jué)faint,loose consiousness.
consiousness,his,her,its,their, ka(嘉 jiā)good,fine,beautiful,praise
praise,commend, yu(猷 yóu)plan,way,depict,scheme,project.


176.    ben     ki     shi    shoku

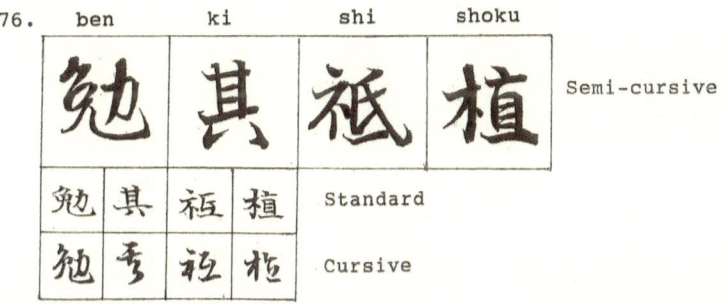

Semi-cursive / Standard / Cursive

Please endeavor to respect and carry out the plan, it would
improve. The good project means " Loyalty and final piety "
( chuko 忠孝 zhong xiao ). This is the way of success in life.
ben(勉 mian)study,devote oneself to,encourage, ki(其 qí)that,its,
he,she,they,his,their,such,secondary, shi(祗 qi)exactly,very,
god of the earth, shoku(植 zhí)plant,grow,set up,establish.

177.  sei    kyu    ki    kai

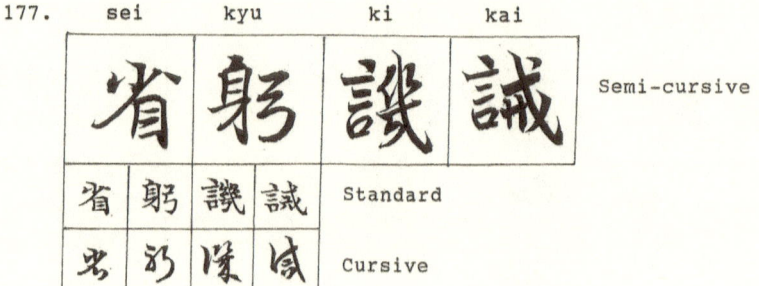

A noble man reflects on himself and warns him against one's slander.  sei(省 shěng)save,omit,economize,leave out,abbreviation, kyu(躬 gōng)body,oneself,by oneself,bow,personally, ki(譏 jī)mock, satirize,investigate,ridicule, kai(誡 jiè)warn,admonish,Commandment.


178.  cho    zo    ko    kyoku

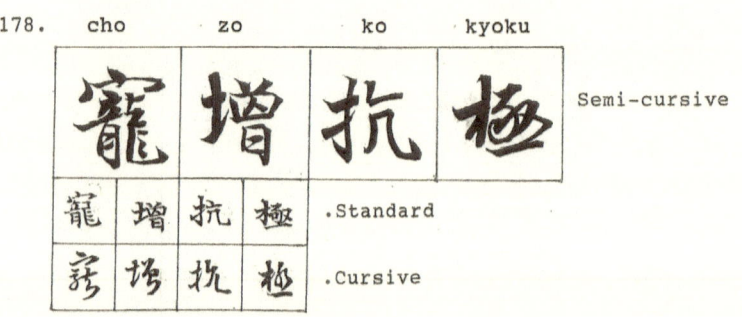

If a noble man's love increases, he will help to decrease the person's suffering. We must control our emotional feeling.
cho(寵 chǒng)dote on,bestow on, zo(增 zēng)increase,gain,add, ko(抗 kàng)resist,combat,fight,refuse,defy,contend with, kyoku(極 jí) pole,the utmost point,the highest degree.

179. tai joku kin chi

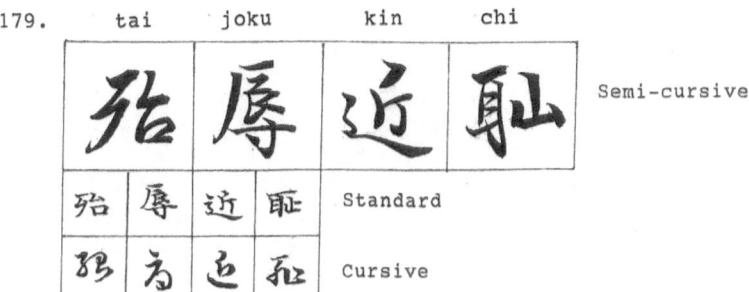

Semi-cursive / Standard / Cursive

When a noble man's love increases, people burn with jealousy. The person who is loved by the noble man is afraid of insult and shame. tai(殆 dài)dangerous,nearly,almost,perilous, joku(辱 rǔ)disgrace,dishonour, kin(近 jìn)near,close,approarching,intimate, chi(恥 chǐ)shame,disgrace,humiliation.

180. rin ko ko soku

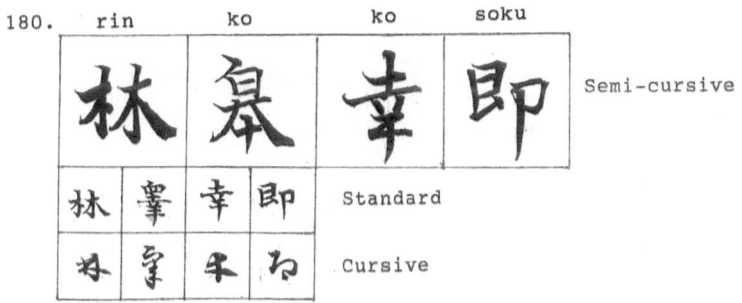

Semi-cursive / Standard / Cursive

The person should reside in the open air in order to escape from misfortune of the city, even after he will be able to enjoy the rest of his life. rin(林 lín)forest,grove,a surname, ko(皋 gāo)highland on the banks of a river, ko(幸 xìng)fortune,lucky,rejoice,hope, soku(即 jí)promptly,at once,reach,be near,assume,namely,even if.

181.  ryo    so    ken    ki

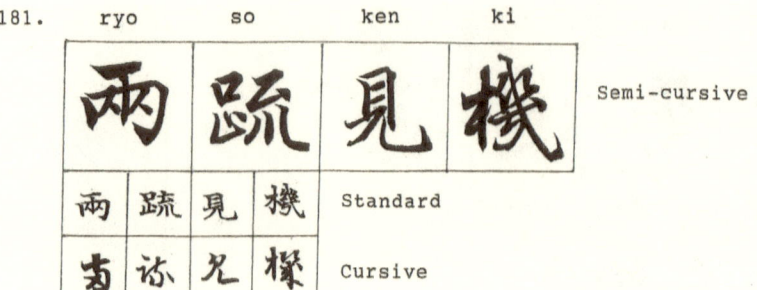

Both of So(soko 疎廣 shū guǎng) and soju(疎受 shū shòu): father and son found the chance to retire : it means to undo the cords( strings ) of the crown. I wonder who could hurt(scare) them.
ryo(兩 liǎng)two,both,either,a few,some, so(疎 shu)thin,sparse, scattered, ken(見 jiàn)see,meet with,refer to,call on,appear, ki(機 jī)machine,engine,aircraft,plane,crucial point,chance, organic,flexible.


182.  kai    so    sui    hyoku

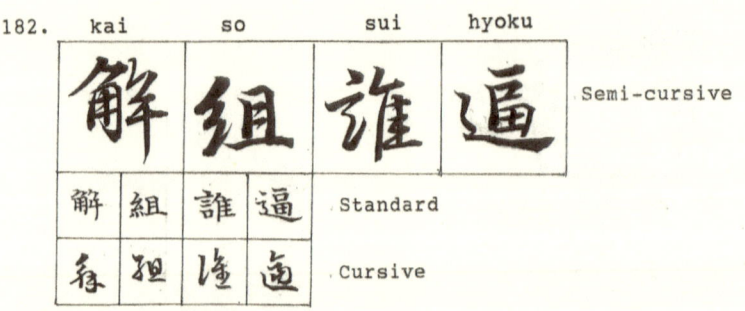

It means to undo the cords( strings ) of the crown.
I wonder who could hurt( scare ) them.
kai(解 jié)separate,untie,undo,allay,dispel, so(組 zǔ)group,set, strings,form,organize, sui(誰 shéi)who,someone,everyone,whoever, kyoku(逼 bī)approach,force,press,compel,extort.

183.  saku   kyo   kan   sho

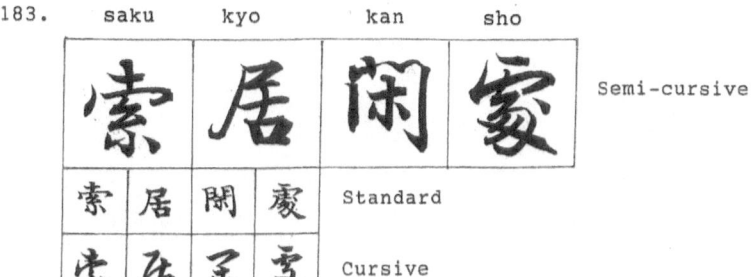

Semi-cursive

Standard

Cursive

The persons like Soko and Soju lived in the calm place and were
separated from the people.  saku(索 suǒ)large rope,look for,
kyo(居 jū)reside,dwell,house,occupy a place,a surname,residence,
kan(閑 xián)spare,free time,not busy,leisure, sho(處 chū)place,
another place,everywhere,point,office,department.


184.  chin   moku   seki   ryo

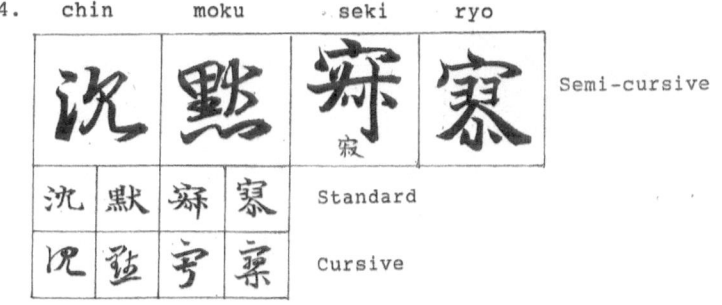

Semi-cursive

寂

Standard

Cursive

They remained in silence and enjoyed living in a peaceful and
happy life.  chin(沈 chén)sink,deep,lower,heavy,feel heavy,
moku(默 mò)quiet,silent,tacit,write from memory,(chinmoku)silence,
seki(寂 jí)still,quiet,silent,lonely,solitary, ryo(寥 liáo)few,
silent,scanty,deserted.

185. kyo    ko    jin    ron

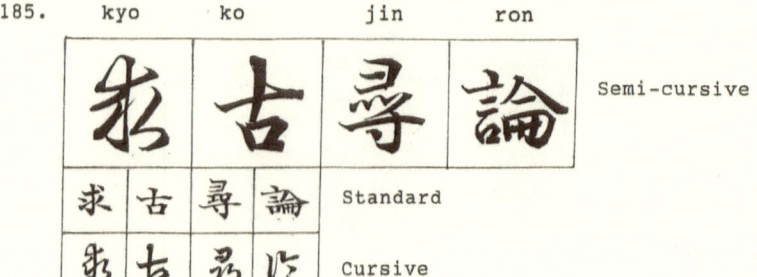

Semi-cursive  
Standard  
Cursive

Men sought for old books and argued with people the contents of the books. kyu(求 qiú)seek,try,strive for,request,beg,entreat,demand, ko(古 gǔ)ancient,old,paleo- ,a surname, jin(尋 xún)seek,look for,search,an ancient measure of length ex. shaku(尺 chǐ), ron(論 lùn)discuss,talk about,view,opinion,statement,determine,according to.

186. san    ryo    sho    yo

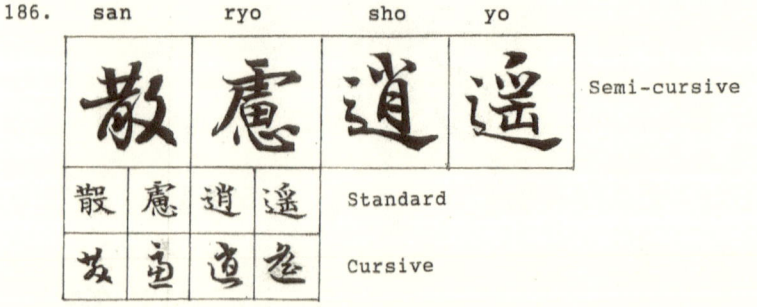

Semi-cursive  
Standard  
Cursive

They pondered freely thoughtful ideas.
san(散 sàn,sǎn)break up,come loose,disperse,distribute,let out,sack,dispel,spread,fall apart,medical powder, ryo(慮 lù)consider,ponder,think over,concern,be anxious,worry, sho(逍 xiāo)wander around,free and unfettered, yo(遥 yáo)distant,remote,far.

187.  kin    so    rui    ken

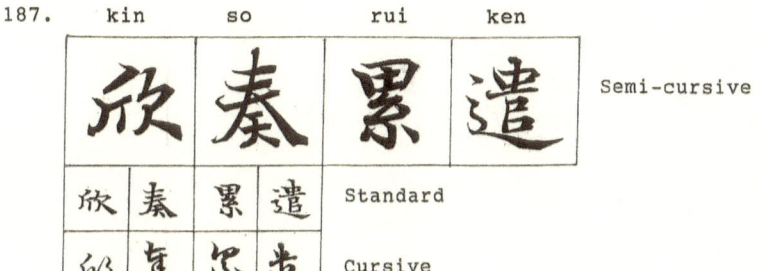

Semi-cursive

Standard

Cursive

Pleasure comes and when troublesome things are over.
kin(欣 xīn)glad,happy,joyful, so(奏 zòu)play music,perform,
achieve,produce, rui(累 lèi)pile up,very often,one after another,
(累 lèi)tired,worry,ask,weary,wear out, ken(遣 qián)dispatch,
dispel,expel,leave.


188.  seki    sha    kan    sho

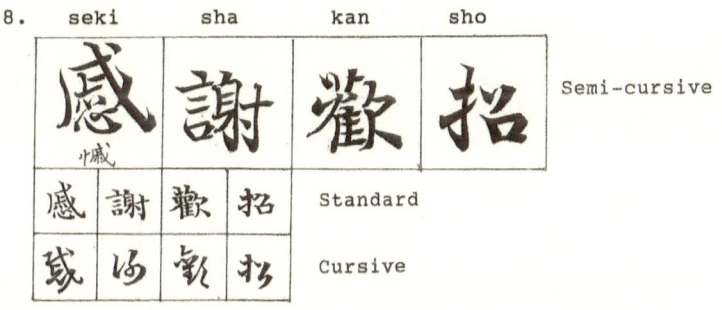

Semi-cursive

Standard

Cursive

After sadness leaves, enjoyment will be invited.
This is called " Carma ".  seki(感 qī)sorrow,relative,a surname,
woe, cry,  an axe-like weapon used in ancient China, sha(謝 xiè)
thank,make an apology,decline,wither of flowers,leaves, kan(歡
huān)joyous,merry,jubilant,vigorously, sho(招 zhāo)beckon,recruit,
invite,tease,provoke,infect,attract,enrol,enlist.

189.  kyo  ka  teki  reki

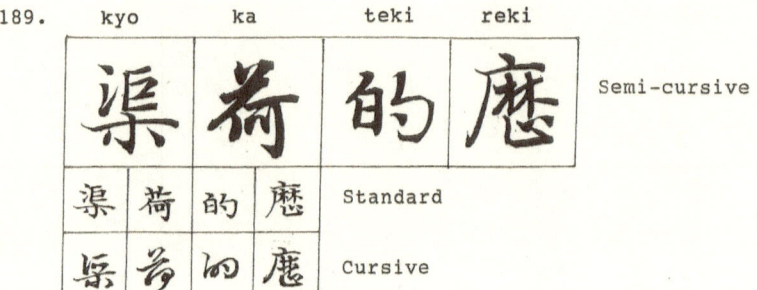

Semi-cursive

Standard

Cursive

Lotus flowers in the gutter of the house are in bloom brilliantly. kyo(渠 qú)canal,ditch,big,great,channel, ka(荷 hé)lotus, teki(的 dì)target,surely,bulls-eye, reki(歷 lì)calendar,go through, undergo,experience,one by one,covering all,all previous sessions.

Tekireki( 的歷 dì lì)brightness,brilliantly.

190.  en  bo  chu  jo

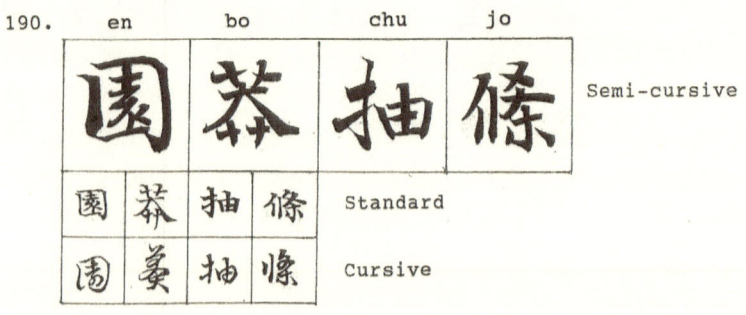

Semi-cursive

Standard

Cursive

The weeds of the garden are pulled out and tree branches grow dense.  en(園 yuán)garden,an area of land for growing plants, a place for public recreation, bo(莽 mǎng)rash,huge,large,grassy, chu(抽 chōu)pull out,pull,bush,take a part from a whole, jo(條 tiáo)twig,a long narrow piece,strip,article,a brief formal note.

191.

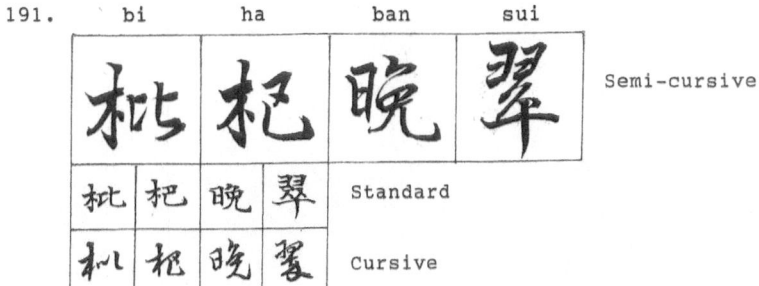

Biwa(枇杷 pí pá)loquat's leaves keep being green for a long time.
bi(枇 pi)loquat, ha(杷 pá)implement,tool,pull,review, ban(晚 wǎn)
evening,night,late,get dark,younger,night comes, sui(翠 cuì)green,
kingfisher,emerald green,jade.

192.

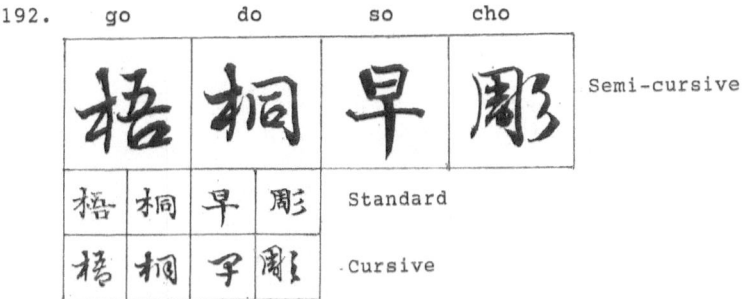

A paulownia tree( godo 梧桐 wú tóng) leaves soon wither and fall
in the autumn. go(梧 wú)Chinese parasol tree,phoenix tree,
do(桐 tóng)paulownia,zither,Chinese parasol tree,tung oil tree,
so(早 zǎo)early morning,long ago,early,soon,in advance,beforehand,
cho(彫 diāo)wither.

Leaves of a paulownia fall, we know the sign of the autumn.
( a proverb from " The book of many flowers: Beauties(Gunhofu
郡芳譜 qún fāng pǔ).

193.

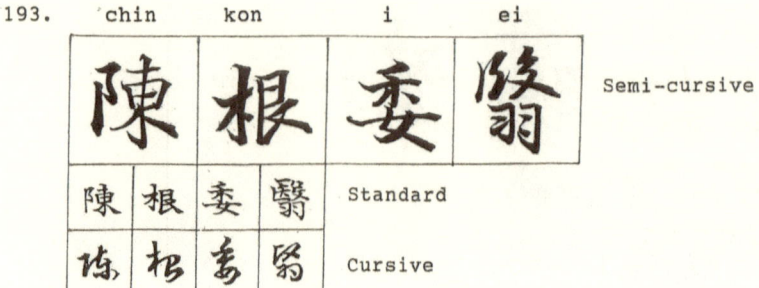

The old tree roots wither and die naturally and grow new ones.
chin(陳 chén)layout,put on display,old,explain,the Chen Dynasty 557 - 589, kon(根 gēn)root,descendants,radical,foot,base,offspring, cause,origin, i(委 wěi)pile,throw away,depend on,detailed, ei(翳 yì)silk cover,screen,conceal,support,the name of a bird.

194.

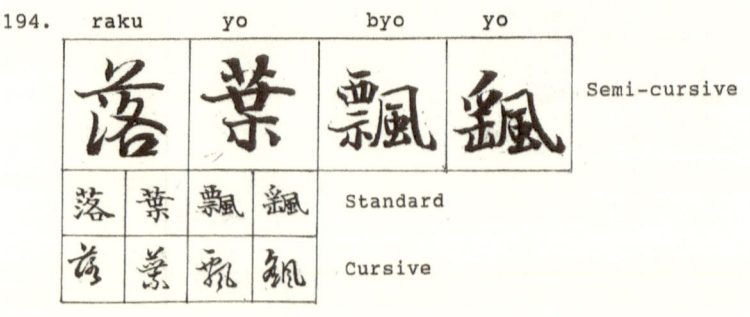

A tree leaves whirl in the wind and fall.
raku(落 lào)fall,drop,go down,set,lower,decline,sink,rest with, yo(葉 yè)leaf,foliage,end, generation, a surname, byo(飄 piāo) whirlwind,wave to,come around,float in the air, yo(飆 yáo) whirl in the wind,shake.

195.　　yu　　　kon　　　doku　　　un

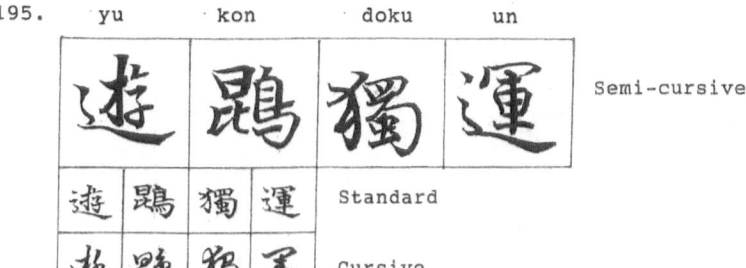

Semi-cursive
Standard
Cursive

The man( soshi 莊子 zhuāng zǐ) plays with a big bird( phoenix ). The bird flies around in the sky.　yu(遊 yóu)play,associate with, reach,roving,rove around,swim, kon(鵾 kūn)a kind of rooster, bamboo cage for transporting chickens or criminals, doku(獨 dú) only,single,solely,alone,old people without offspring,standoffish, un(運 yùn)fortune,motion,movement,carry,transport,luck,fate.

196.　　ryo　　　ma　　　ko　　　sho

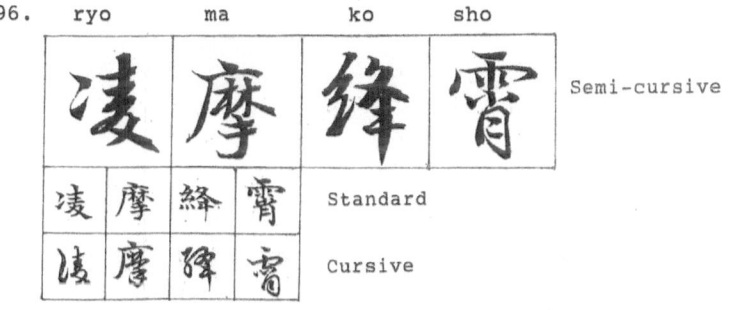

Semi-cursive
Standard
Cursive

The man means a retired person. A retired person enjoys himself in the countryside like a big bird. The word of kon(鵾 kūn) has a meaning of a big fish( taigyo 大魚 dà yú) and changed to a big bird( otori 大鳥 dà niǎo). The idea came from Soshi( 莊子 zhuang zi)" Nankashinkyo 南華真経 nan hua zhen jing " by Soshyu( 莊周 zhuang zhou ).　ryo(凌 líng)approach,ice in block,get on, tower aloft,fear, ma(摩 mó)rub,scrape,study,mull over,gently stroke, ko(絳 jiàng)deep red,crimson, sho(霄 xiāo)sleet,clouds,fade away, early evening,night,die out,go out,disappear.

197.  tan    doku    gan    shi

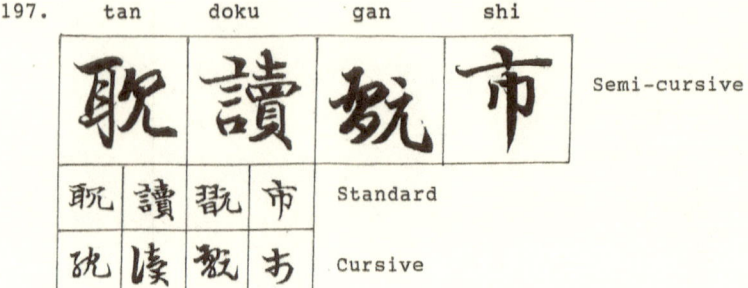

Semi-cursive
Standard
Cursive

One tends to indulge in reading books, therefore he goes to the
bookstore in the city and devours the stories of the books.
tan(耽 dān)abandon oneself to,indulge in,enjoy,one has big earlobes,
deep, doku(讀 dú)read,read aloud,attend school, gan(翫 wàn)enjoy,
treat lightly,appreciate,play,have fun,amuse oneself with, shi(市
shì)city,market,buy or sell,municipality.


198.  gu    moku    no    so

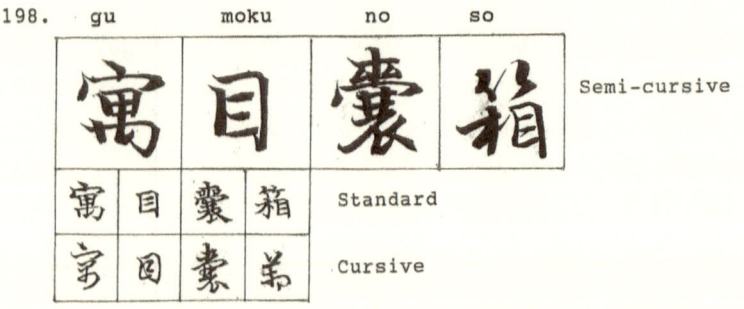

Semi-cursive
Standard
Cursive

Because he is poor and is unable to buy any books. To look over
a bag and boxes means to indulge in reading books.
gu(寓 yù)reside,live,abide,imply,contain, me (目 mù)eye,look,
regard,order,catalogue,table of contents, no(囊 náng)bag,pocket,
purse,wrap,all, so(箱 xiāng)chest,box,case,trunk,anything in the
shape of a box.

199.

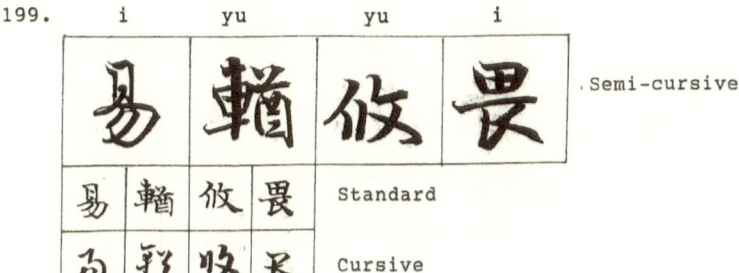

To be more careful about my words and deeds is very important.
i(易 yì)easy,despise,change,exchange,fortune telling,a surname,
yu(輶 yóu)light,a light weight carriage, yu(攸 yōu)place,easy,
far away,relaxed, i(畏 wèi)fear,respect,be stiff.


200.

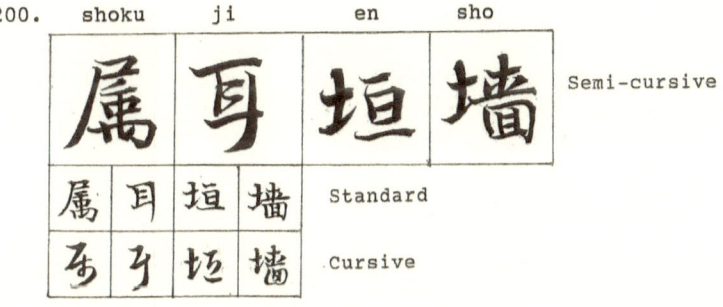

Noblemen think that someone is behind the fence and never uses
careless expressions.   shoku(属 shǔ)stretch,line,category,be,
belong to,family members,be subordinate, ji(耳 ěr)ear,just,only,
en(垣 yuán)wall,fence,project,city,public office,a star name,
sho(墙 qiáng)wall,fence,cloth for a coffin,border.

201.  gu    zen    san    han

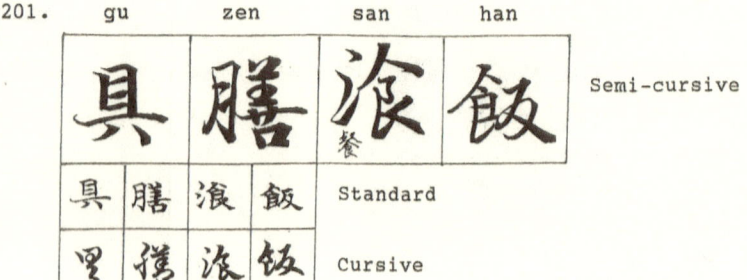

Semi-cursive

Standard

Cursive

One prepares a meal and eats the meal.
gu(具 jù)prepare,tool,utensil,certain instruments or machines, implement,dead bodies, zen(膳 shàn)meal,board, san(湌 cān)eat, food,meal, han(飯 fàn)cooked rice or other cerial,meal.


202.  teki    ko    ju    cho

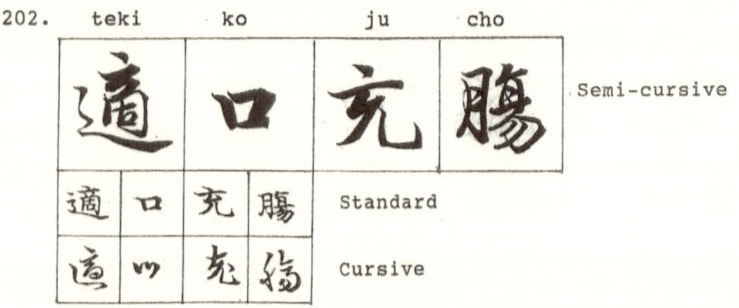

Semi-cursive

Standard

Cursive

If the food is just a right portion, it makes one's stomach satisfied. Rongo(論語 lùn yǔ)" the Analects of Confucius " included a proverb : Noblemen never eat overly refind food, they are satisfied to eat ordinary food. teki(適 shì)follow,go, pursue,fit,suitable,just,right,well,comfortable, ko(口 kǒu)mouth, opening,entrance,a gateway of the Great Wall,hole,cut,the edge of knife, ju(充 chōng)sufficient,full,fill,act as,serve as,stuff, fuku(腸 fù)belly of the body,mind,idea,front,warmth.

203.   ho      yo      ho      sai

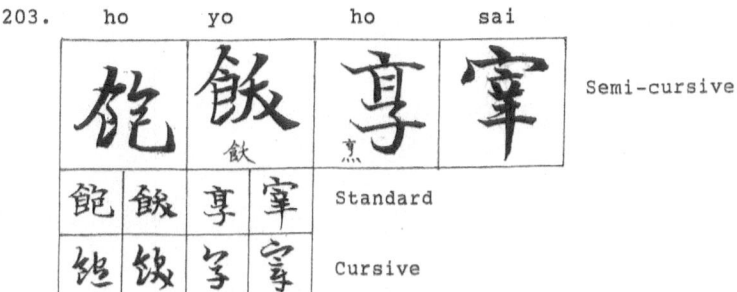

If one gets tired of a meat hot pot dish, he does not want to have just any kind of good food. ho(飽 bǎo)get tired of,satisfy, yo(飫 yù)feast,daily food,get tired of,to be given, ho(亨 pēng) boil,cook in water,brew,fry quickly in hot oil and stir in sauce, sai(宰 zǎi)cook,organize,head,chief,minister,tomb.

204.   ki      en      so      ko

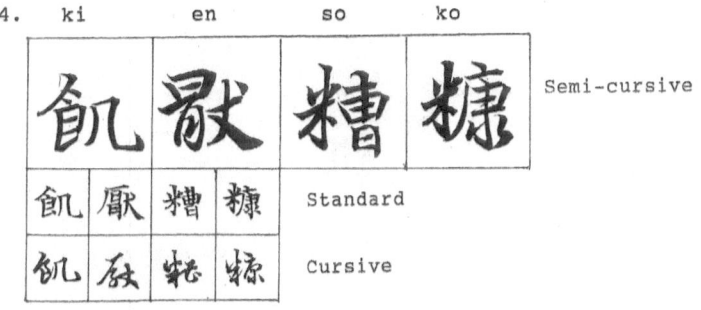

When someone is hungry, he is able to eat anything even though the dish is not delicious. The food is like rice-bran in lees. Common people are unable to eat the food. ki(飢 jī)hungry,starved, famine, en(厭 yàn)be tired of,follow,calm,push,detest,hide, so(糟 zāo)lees,cheap, ko(糠 kāng)chaff,bran,husk,spongy.

205.  shin    seki    ko    kyu

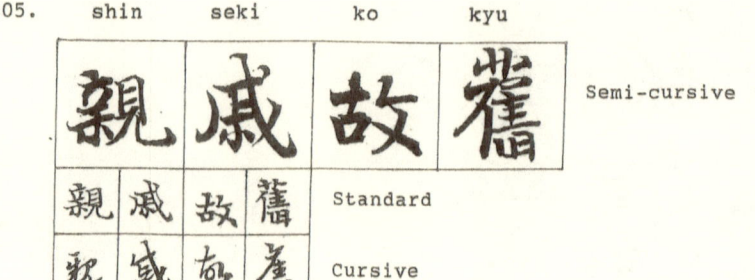

Semi-cursive

Standard

Cursive

One makes friends with his relatives like old friends.
shin(親 qīn)relatives,friend,parents,new,parent,seki(戚
qī)relative,(qī)a surname,sorrow,woe,an axe-like weapon used
in ancient China, ko(故 gù)former,old,friend,die,aquaintance,
kyu(舊 jìu)past,old,used,worn,bygone,onetime.


206.   ro    sho    i    ryo

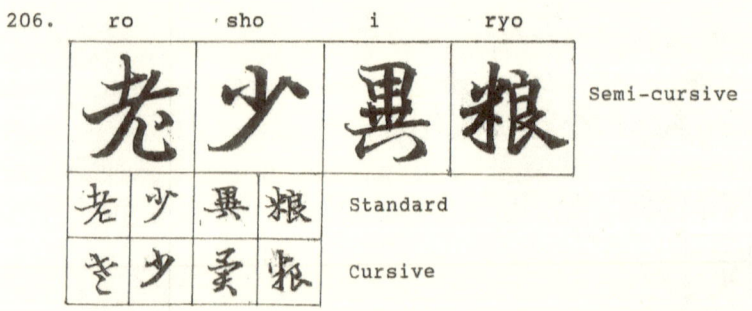

Semi-cursive

Standard

Cursive

An old man is physically weak, so, he must have a substatial meal,
but younsters are able to eat simple meal. ro(老 lǎo)old people,
experienced,veteran,dark(color)very, sho(少 shǎo)few,little,less,
lack,lose,a moment,a little while,stop,quit, i(異 yì)different,
strange,unusual,extraordinary,other,another,surprise,separate,
ryo(粮 liáng)grain,food,provisions,grain tax paid in kind.

207.

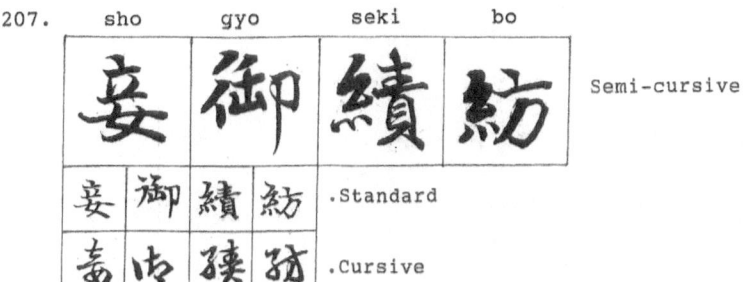

A concubine ought to use spinning a wheel.
sho(妾qiè)concubine,kept mistress, gyo(御yù)manage,control,
drive a carriage,imperial,resist,keep out, seki(績jī)achievement,
merit,twist hempen thread, bo(紡bǎng)spin,thread.

208.

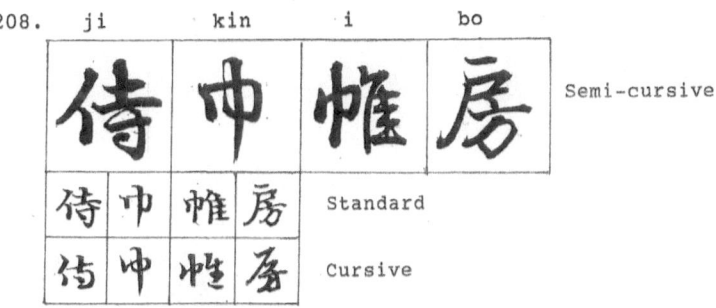

She put on a hood and wait for her husband in darkening the room
by window curtains. ji(侍shì)wait upon,serve,attend upon,retinue,
kin(巾jīn)a piece of cloth as used for a towel,scarf,handkerchief,
i(帷wéi)bed-curtain,cover, bo(房fáng)house,bedroom and a living
room,nest,a tuft,a fringe,a bunch.

209. gan    sen    en    ketsu

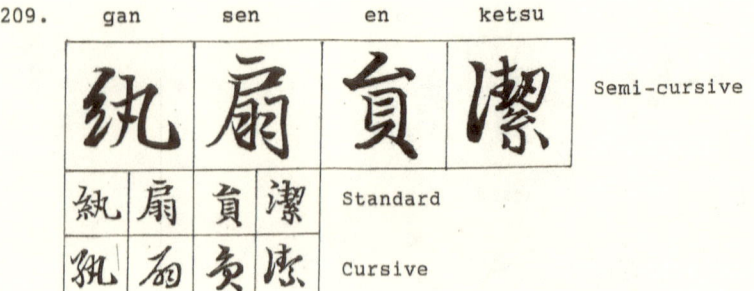

Semi-cursive

Standard

Cursive

Gansen(紈扇 wán shan) silk made fans are rounded and white.
Gansen are made in Sei(齊 qí) country 386 B.C. - 221 B.C.
gan(紈 wan)fine silk fabrics, sen(扇 shàn)fan, a sliding, hinged,
leaf, bamboo made doors, windows, en(貟 yuán)round, circular, circle,
tactful, satisfactory, ketsu(潔 jié)clean, pure, brave, gallant.


210. gin    shoku    i    ko

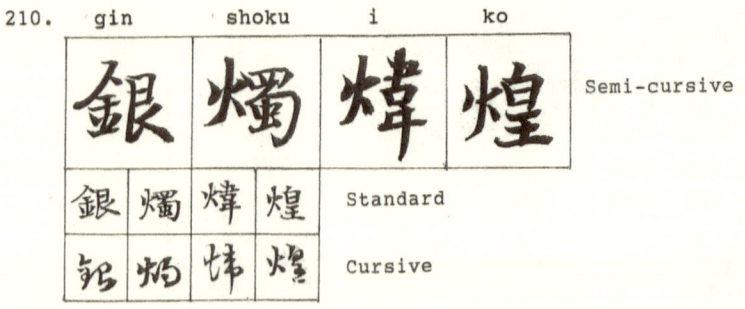

Semi-cursive

Standard

Cursive

A silver made candlestick is shiny and dazzling.
gin(銀 yín)silver, relating to currency or money, silver colored,
shoku(燭 zhú)candle, illuminate, light up, watt, i(煒 wěi)bright,
shine, red, prosperous, ko(煌 huáng)bright, brilliant.

211. chu   min   seki   bi

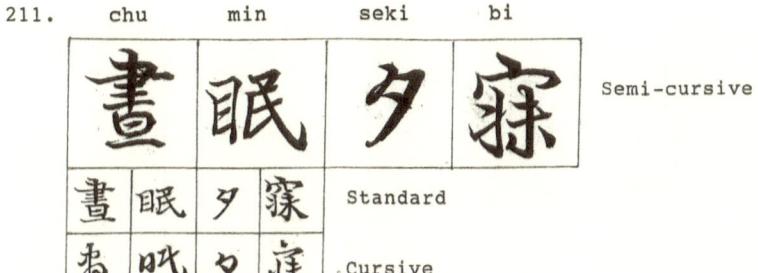

Semi-cursive
Standard
Cursive

If one has a nap during the day time, and sleeps a night, chu(畫,晝 zhòu)day time,daylight,day, min(眠 mían)sleep,to die, go to bed,dormancy, seki(夕 xī)sunset,evening,night, bi(寐 mei) sleep,lie down.


212. ran   jun   zo   sho

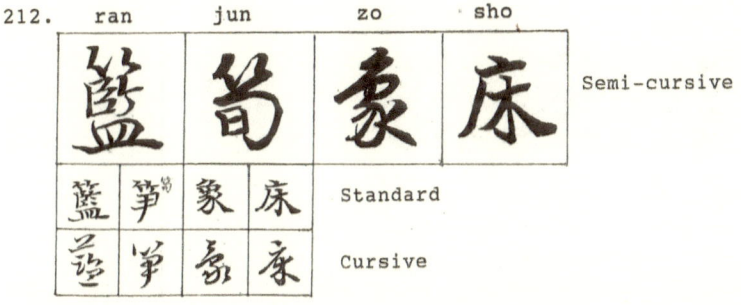

Semi-cursive
Standard
Cursive

on the bed of the blue bamboo-made mat decorated with ivories, one will be able to sleep comfortably. ran(籃 lán)blue,a surname, indigo plant, jun(笋 sǔn)bamboo shoot,bamboo made musical instrument, zo(象 xiàng)elephant,appearance,shape,image,imitate, sho(床 chuáng)bed,shaped like a bed.

213. gen   ka   shu   en

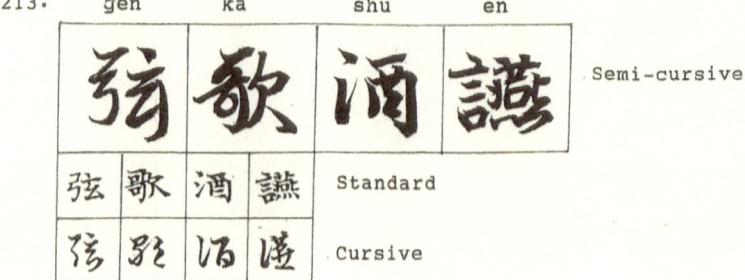

Semi-cursive
Standard
Cursive

Playing musical instrument like a harp or a lute and chanting poems for a drinking party.  gen(絃 xián)bowstring,string, chord(math),hypotenuse, ka(歌 gē)song,sing, shu(酒 jiǔ)wine, alcoholic drink,liquor,spirits,drinking party, en(讌 yàn)feast, entertain at a banquet,fete.


214. setsu   hai   kyo   sho

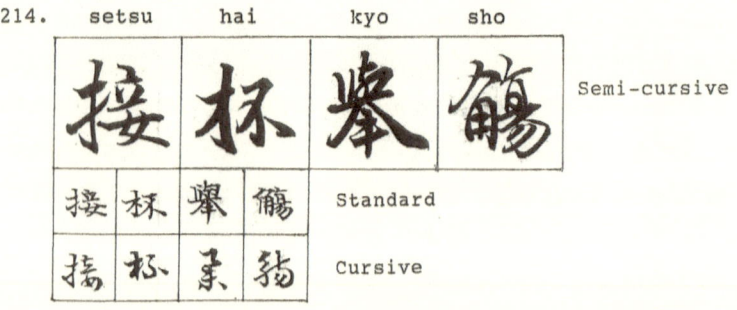

Semi-cursive
Standard
Cursive

Entertaining people by using a sake-cup : offering rice wine and people enjoy the feast.  setsu(接 jiē)meet,welcome,connect, join put together,continue,take over,catch,come close to,receive, hai(杯 bēi)cup,drink,trophy, kyo(舉 jǔ)lift,rase,hold up,act, deed,move,start,elect, sho(觴 shāng)wine up,drinking vessel, sake cup.

215. kyo shu ton soku

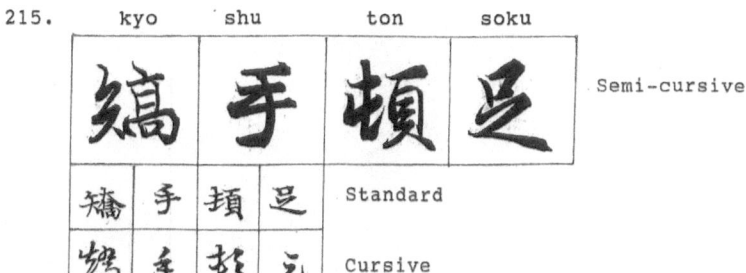

Semi-cursive

Standard

Cursive

By raising hands and fluttering legs, they beat time with their hands. kyo( 矯 jiǎo)pretend,feign,dissemble,rectify,brave,strong, shu( 手 shǒu)hand,hold,handy,personally,for skill, ton(頓 dùn) pause,arrange,tired,fatigued,settle,at once, soku(足 zú)foot,leg, enough,ample,sufficient,fully,as much as.

216. etsu yo sha ko

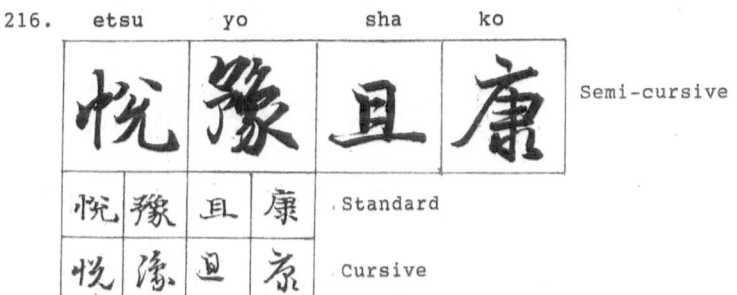

Semi-cursive

Standard

Cursive

It means to enjoy dancing and being peaceful.
This is one of pleasures in life.
etsu(悦 yuè)happy,pleased,delighted,please,delight, yo(豫 yù) beforehand,in advance,enjoy,I, sha(且 qiě)besides,moreover, furthermore,for a little while, ko(康 kāng)well-being,health, a surname.

217.　teki　　ko　　shi　　shoku

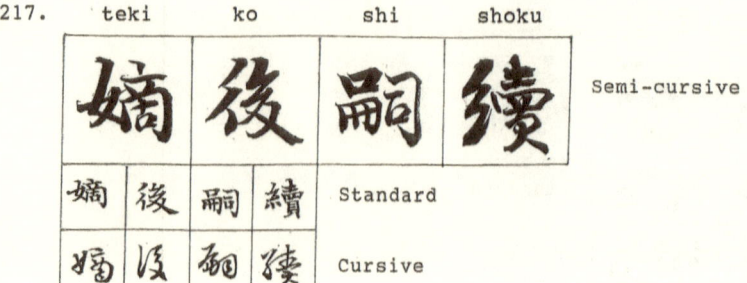

Semi-cursive

Standard

Cursive

The eldest son inherits after the parents pass away and becomes an heir. teki(嫡 dí)the wife's eldest son,lineal descent, closely related, ko(後 hòu)behind,back,rear,after,afterwards, later, shi(嗣 sì)succeed,inherit,heir,descendant, shoku(續 xù) continuous,extend,successive,join,add.


218.　sai　　shi　　jo　　sho

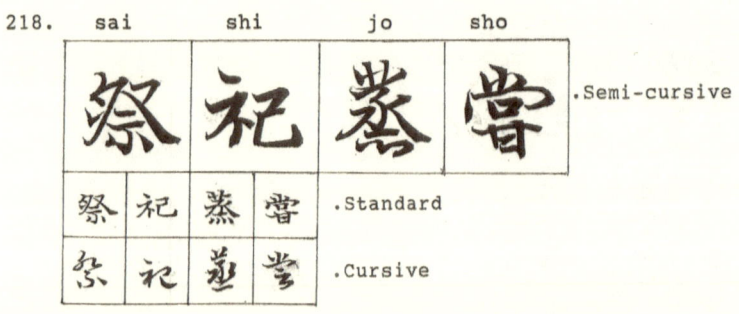

.Semi-cursive

.Standard

.Cursive

He ought to organize the Festivals to pray to ancestries. Saishi(祭祀 jì sì) Festivals are yaku(祠 )spring:the Zhou Dynasty, Tei(禘祠 dì cí)summer, Sho(嘗 cháng)autumn and Jo(蒸 zhēng)winter.  sai(祭 jì)festival,hold a memorial ceremony for, shi(祀 sì)offer sacrifices to the gods,the spirit of the dead, jo(蒸 zhēng)steam,evaporate,blow over,fade away, sho(嘗 嚐 cháng)taste,ever,autumn festival,once.

219.

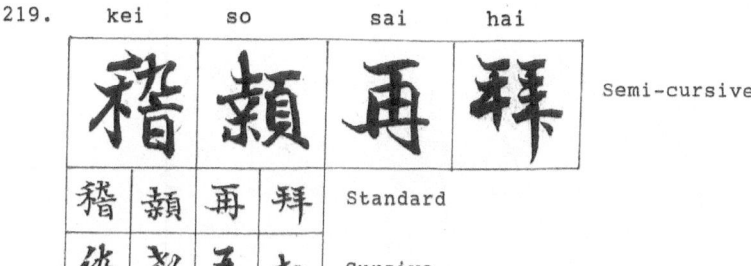

One must pray to the ancestries during the festival, first
touch his forehead on the ground and then bow twice respectfully.
kei(稽 jī)check,examine,investigate,consider,save,dispute,argue,
so(顙 sǎng)forehead, sai(再 zài)again,once more,further,in addition,
hai(拜 bài)do obeisance,congratulate,visit.

220.

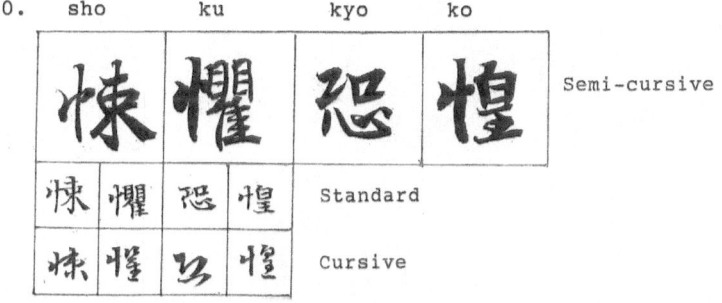

Afterwad one has to dedicate to his ancestries with one's modest
behavior. sho(悚 sǒng)terrified,horrified, ku(懼 jù)fear,dread,
kyo(恐 kǒng)fear,intimidate,terrify,dread, ko(惶 huáng)anxiety,
fear,trepidation.

221.  sen  cho  kan  yo

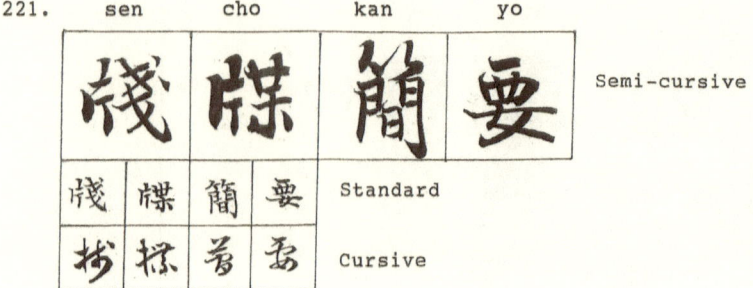

Semi-cursive

Standard

Cursive

Letters and tallies must be short( summarized ).
sen(牋 jiān)letter,tally,writing paper,annotation, cho(牒 dié)
an official document or note,certificate,lineage,genealogy,
kan(簡 jiǎn)bamboo slip used for writing on in ancient times,
letter,simple,brief,select,choose, yo(要 yào)want,ask for,wish,
main point,essentials,important,must,should,be going to,want to.


222.  ko  to  shin  sho

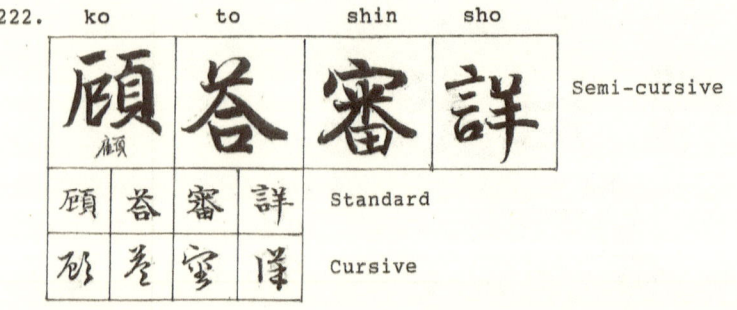

Semi-cursive

Standard

Cursive

Replying to one's letter should be in minute detail.
ko(顧 gù)turn round and look at,visit,call on,attend to,customer,
a surname, to(答 dá)answer,reply,respond,return,reciprocate,
shin(審 shěn)detail,careful,meticulous,examine,try,interrogate,
know,indeed,really, sho(詳 xiáng)detailed,minute,details,know
clearly,particulars.

223.

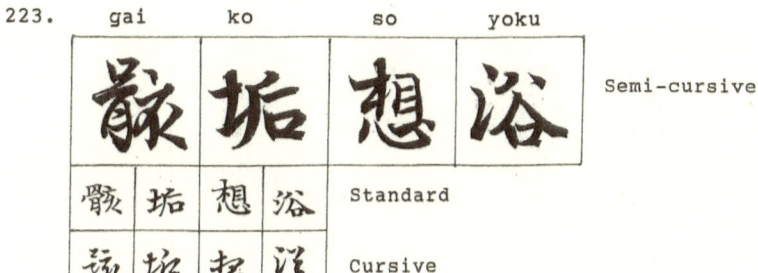

If your body is covered with dirt, you will think about bathing.
gai(骸 hái)body,corpse,bones of the body,skeleton,bones of the dead, ko(垢 gòu)dirty,filthy,disgrace,humiliation, so(想 xiǎng)think,ponder,suppose,consider,want to,miss, yoku(浴 yù)bath,bathe.

224.

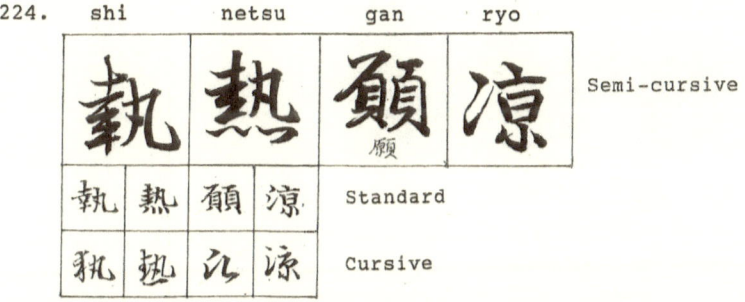

Avoiding the heat, one wishes it will be cool.
(Proverb) If you can not stand the heat, go out of the kitchen.
" President Truman's way of saying: 33rd President 1945 - 1953.

shu(執 zhí)hold,grasp,direct,manage,persist,stick to one's views, netsu(熱 rè)heat,hot,heat up,fever,temperature,ardent,warmhearted, fad, gan(願 yuàn)hope,wish,desire,be willing,be ready, ryo(凉 liáng)cool,cold,discourage.

225.

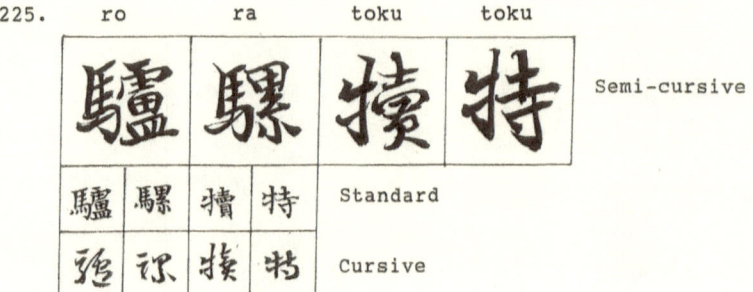

Donky(ro 驢 lú) and mule(ra 騾 luó). Calf(toku 犢 dú) and bull(toku te). toku(特 tè)bull,special,unusual,exceptional,very.


226.

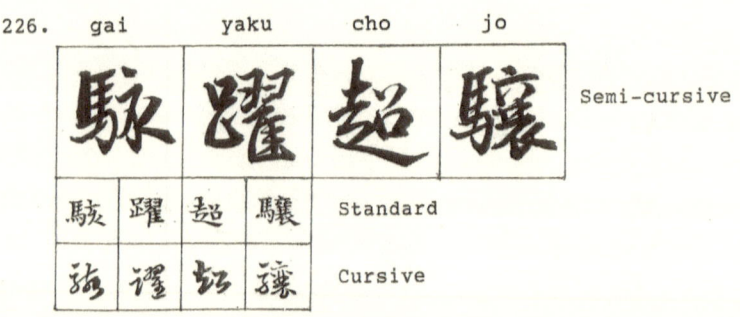

When they are shocked, run fast, jump over the fence.However, human beings should not take that way. Observe everything carefully, act as a modest person.  gai(駭 hài)be astonished, be shocked, yaku(躍 yuè)leap,jump, cho(超 chāo)exceed,surpass, overtake,super,extra,transcend,go beyond,jo(驤 xiāng)gallop, rear one's head,go up,run.

227.  chu    zan    zoku    to

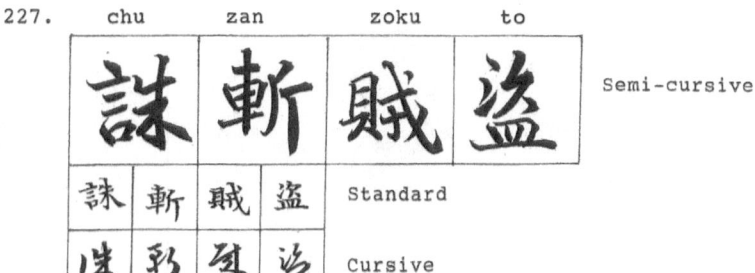

Thieves and robbers must be killed,
chu(誅 zhū)punish,put a criminal to death, zan(斬 zhǎn)cut,chop,
endure,very, zoku(賊 zéi)thief,traitor,enemy,sly,cunning,crafty,
evil, to(盜 dao)steal,rob,thief,robber.


228.  ho    kaku    han    bo

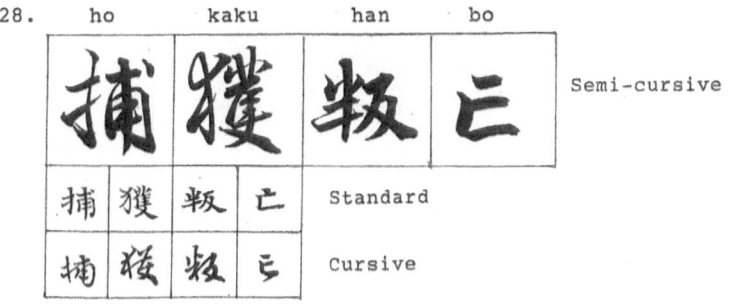

and also traitors, fugitives should be punished by only this
way, we are able to maintain social order.  ho(捕 bǔ)catch,seize,
arrest, kaku(獲 huò)capture,catch, han(叛 pàn)betray,rebel against,
bo(亡 wáng)flee,run away,lose,die,deceased,perish,subjugate,
conquer.

229.    fu      sha     ryo     gan

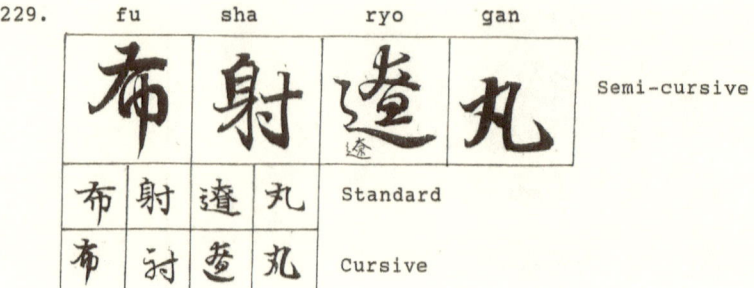

Semi-cursive

Standard

Cursive

Rofu(呂布 lǔ bù) is the master of shooting arrows. Giryo(宜遼 yí liáo) is very skillful in juggling with children's beanbags(balls). fu(布 bu)cotton cloth,cloth,an ancient coin,tax,spread, arrange,describe,distribute,spread, sha(射 shè)shoot,fire, insinuate,discharge in a jet,send out light or heat, ryo(遼 líao) distant,far away,the Liao Dynasty 907 - 1125, gan(丸 wán)ball, pellet,pill,bolus.


230.    kei     kin     gen     sho

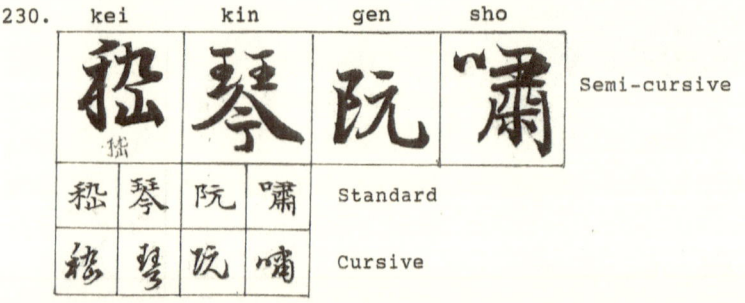

Semi-cursive

Standard

Cursive

Keiko(嵇康 jī kāng) is the expert of playing a traditional zither. Genseki(阮藉 ruan jie) is also master of recitation of poems. These people are outstanding in an art and will live forever in our memory. Keiko(嵇康 ji kang = oya 叔夜 shú yè) kei(嵇 ji)a surname,the name of mountain(Henan Province), kin(琴 qín)general name for certain musical instruments,a seven-stringed plucked instrument in some ways similar to the zither, gen(阮 ruǎn)the name of musical instruments,the name of country,a surname, sho(嘯 xiāo)make a whistling sound,give a long,loud cry,whistle, howl,roar.

231.  ten    pitsu    rin    shi

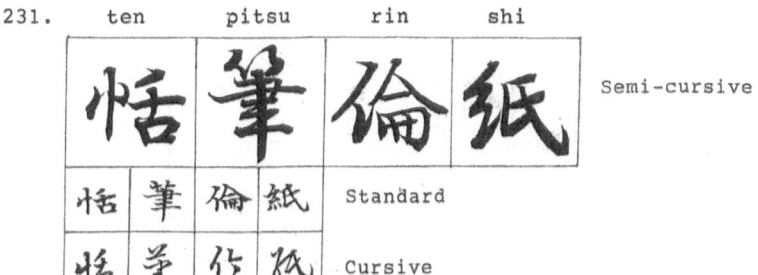

Moten(蒙恬 méng tiang) created a brush with rabbit hair.
Sairin(蔡倫 cai lun = Keichu 敬仲 jìng zhòng) produced paper
for the first time.  ten(恬 tián)quiet,calm,tranquil,not care at all,
remain unperturbed, pitsu(筆 bǐ)writing brush,pen,pencil,stroke,
touch,technique of writing, rin(倫 lún)human relations,way,peer,
match,logic,order, shi(紙 zhī)paper.


232.  kin    ko    jin    cho

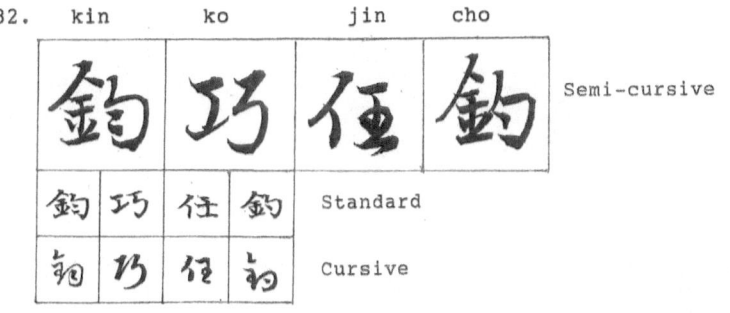

Bakin(馬鈞 ma jun) created a cart with a wooden toy pointing
toward south(shinansha 指南車 zhǐ nán chē). Jinko(任公 ren gong)
is the master of fishing. The craftmanship of these people is
extremely good.  kin(鈞 jūn)ancient unit of weight,you to seniors
or superiors, ko(巧 qiǎo)skillful,clever,cunning,artful,deceitful,
opportune,coincidental, jin(任 rén)give,assign,appoint,undertake,
let allow, cho(釣 diào)fish with a hook and line,angle(fishing),
pursure.

233.　shaku　　fun　　ri　　zoku

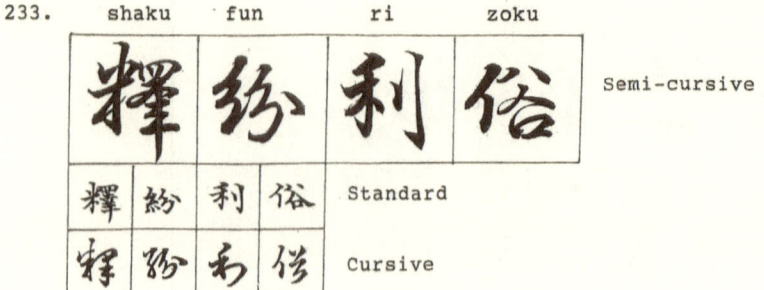

Semi-cursive

Standard

Cursive

They corrected a social confusion, and gave the common people convenience. shaku(釋 shì)shoot an arrow, elucidate, explain, let go, release, set free, fun(紛 fēn)confused, tangled, disorderly, ri(利 lì)advantage, sharp, profit, interest, benefit, zoku(俗 sú)custom, common, popular, convention, lay, secular, vulgar.

234.　hei　　kai　　ka　　myo

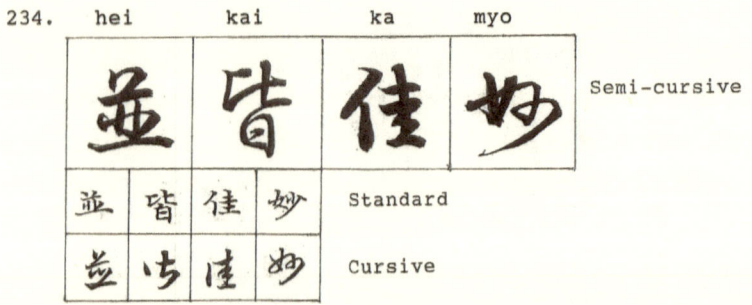

Semi-cursive

Standard

Cursive

The above-mentioned 8 people are equally super good. hei(並 bìng)equally, stand or place side by side, kai(皆 jiē)all, each and every, ka(佳 jiā)good, fine, beautiful, myo(妙 miào)fine, wonderful, excellent, subtle, clever, ingenious.

235.

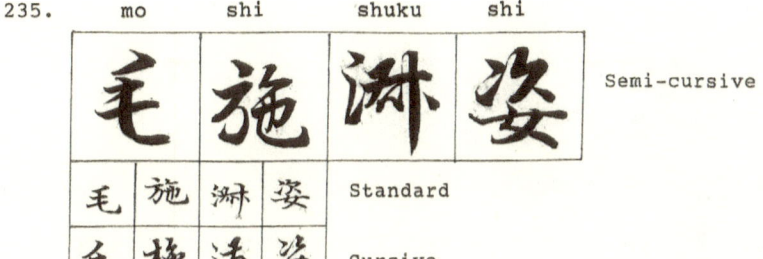

Mosho(毛嬙 máo qiáng: go 吳 wu country) and Seishi( 西施 xī shī:
Etsu 越 yue country) are good and beauty.  mo(毛 máo)hair,feather,
down,wool,mildew,mould,gross,little,a surname, shi(施 shi)use,
apply,bestow,hand out,impose,excute,carry out, shuku(淑 shú)
refined,pure,virtuous,lovely,beautiful, shi(姿 zī)looks,gesture,
appearance,carriage,posture.


236.

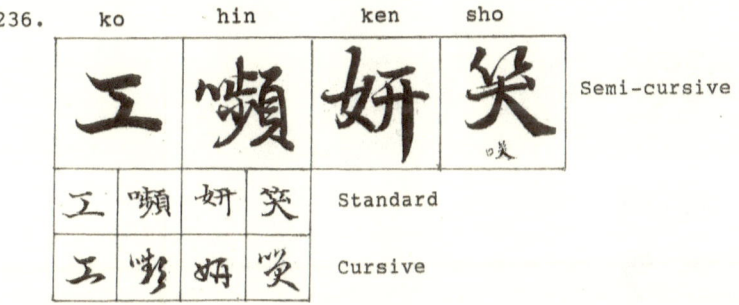

When Mo and Shi knit their brows, they are beautiful and it
makes the common people sexually aroused with smiles. ko(工
gōng)be good at,work,meritorious deed,labour,project,weaving,
hin(顰 pin)knit the brows,frown, ken(妍 pín)beautiful,have illicit
relations with, sho(笑 xiào)smile,laugh,ridicule,laugh at,bloom.

237.

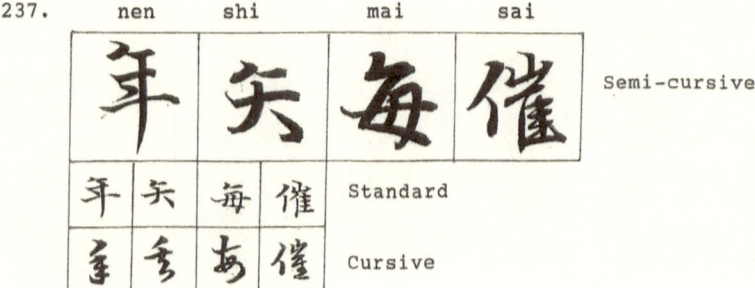

Time flies like an arrow.
nen(年 nián)year,age,annual,yearly,harvest,New Year,a surname,
shi(矢 shǐ)arrow,vow,swear,faces,do,excrement, mai(每 měi)every,
per,each,often,each time,even if, sai(催 cūi)urge,hurry,press,
event,hasten,expedite.

238.

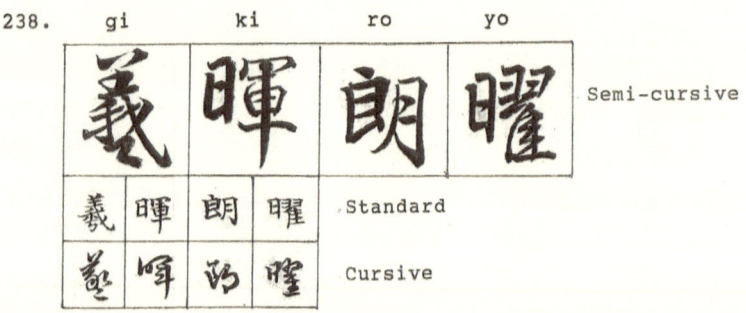

The sunlight is bright, the moonlight is blue light. You must
push yourself to study for training. Time never waits for us.
gi(羲 xī)sunlight,early morning, ki(暉 hūi)brightness,splendour,
ro(朗 lǎng)light,bright,loud and clear,sunny disposition,fine,
yo(曜 yào)shine,sunlight,illuminate,luminary,a week.

239.   sen    ki    ken    atsu

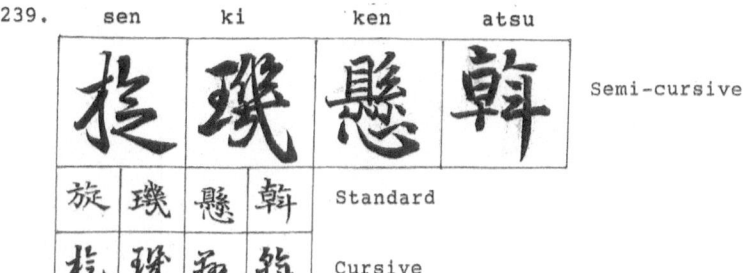

By using the surveying instrument for astronomy, we are able to
see the transition of the moonlight.  sen( 旋 xuán)circle,revolve,
spin,return,come back,soon,whirl, ki(璣 jī)a pearl that is not
quite round,an ancient astronomical instrument,a name of star,
ken( 懸 xuán)hang,suspend,outstanding,feel anxious, atsu( 斡 wò)
revolve,spin,rotate,good office,a handle of the ladle.


240.   kai    haku    kan    sho

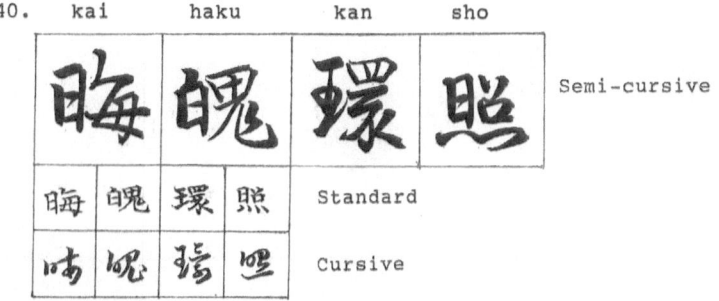

From the last of a lunar month( December ) to on the first day
of the month( in January or February, we know global system.
kai( 晦 hùi)the last day of a lunar month(December),dark,night,
gloomy,obscure, haku( 魄 pò)body,the fresh,soul,spirit,vigour,
kan(環 huán)encircle,link,ring,hoop,surroun, sho( 照 zhào)shine,
light up,reflect,illuminate,mirror,take a picture,permit,photo.

241.    shi    shin    shyu    ko

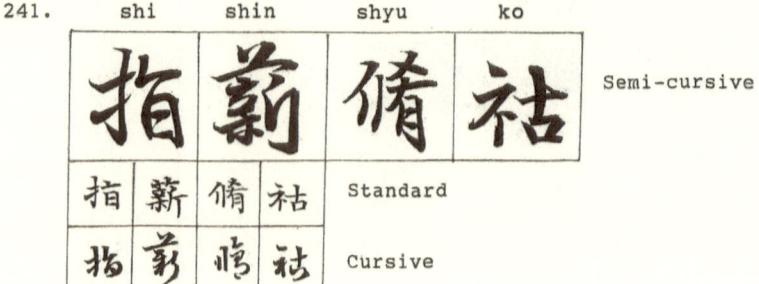

One points out the flaming firewood. If one adds logs, the flame will continue like good deed.  shi(指 zhǐ)finger,point out, degit,count on,depend on,point to, shin(薪 xīn)firewood,salary, faggot, shyu(脩 xiū)dried meat,to dry,study,cultivate,build,mend, write,compile,trim,decorate,a surname, ko(祜 hù)blessing,bliss.


242.    ei    sui    kis    sho

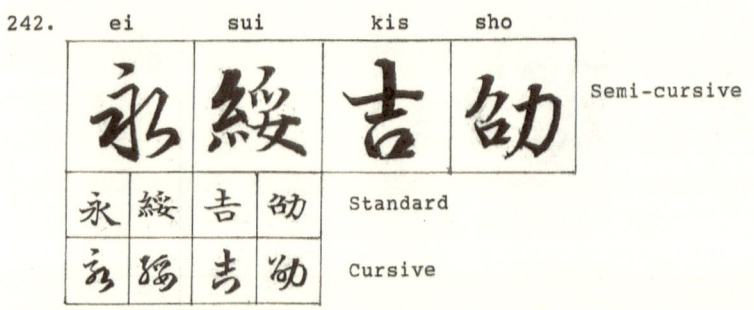

If one shows his goodness, good fortune will be given to him continuously. The person will have longevity.  ei(永 yǒng) forever,always,perpetually, sui(綏 suī)peaceful,pacify, kitsu(吉 jí)lucky,propitious,auspicious, sho(劭 shào)encourage,urge, exhort,excellent: eisui(永綏 yǒng suī)longevity.

243.    ku        ho        in        ryo

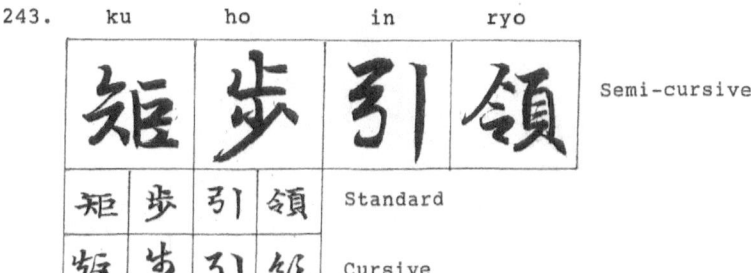

Semi-cursive

Standard

Cursive

There is a rule to walk upright by stretching one's neck.
ku(矩 jǔ)rules,carpenter's square,square,regulations, ho(步 bù)
walk,step,stage,pace,go on foot,condition,situation, in(引 yǐn)
draw,stretch,lead,guide,make,cite, ryo(領 lǐng)neck,collar,
neckband,outline,main point, inryo(引領 yǐn lǐng)stretching
one's neck.


244.    fu        gyo       ro        byo

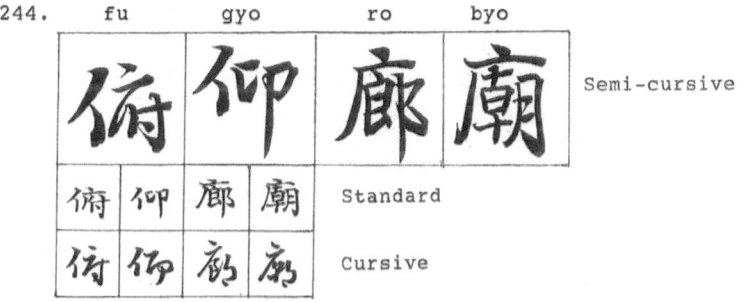

Semi-cursive

Standard

Cursive

Look up to the mausoleum to appease(comfort) the soul of our
ancestries. Behave like being in the palace.   fu(俯 fǔ)look down,
bow one's head,kneel down, gyo(仰 yang)face upward,admire,respect,
look up to, ro(廊 láng)corridor,porch,veranda,eaves, byo(廟 miào)
temple,shrine,palace.

245. soku  tai  kyo  so

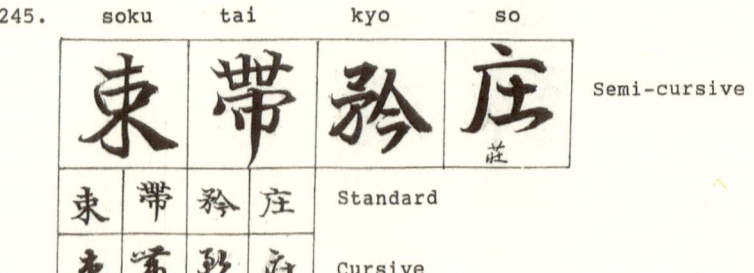

Refrain from conducting careless behaviors. Keep a grave deed. Dressing up when you attend the solemn ceremony. soku(束 shù) a bunch,bundle,bind,be careful,behave oneself prudently,a little, a few minutes, tai(帶 dài)belt,ribbon,band,area,girdle,carry, have,simultanious,lead,look after,snake, kyo(矜 jīn)pity,girdle, sympathize with,conceited,self-important,grave,solemn, so(莊 zhuāng)serious,manor,village,sedate,a surname,a place of business.

246. hai  kai  sen  sho

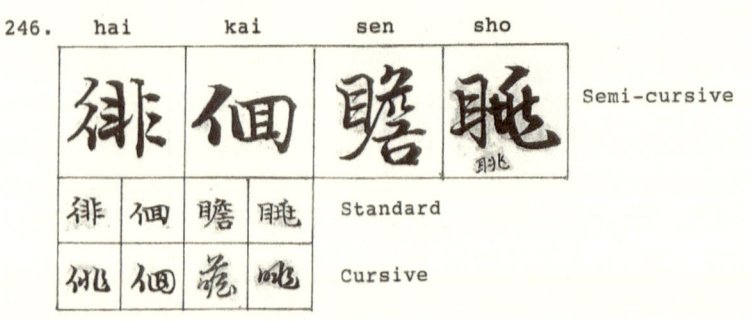

Even though loitering around outside of the palace, you must be careful of expressing an opinion.  hai(俳 pái)wander around, waver,hesitate,pace up and down, kai(佪 huái)wander around,dark, sen(瞻 zhān)look up or forward,look down, sho(眺 tiào)view,look into the distance from a high place.

247.  ko   ro   ka   bun

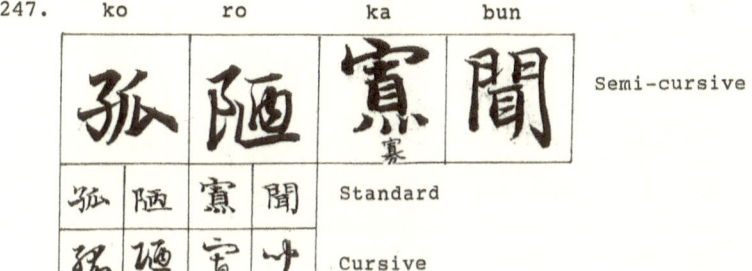

If one hides and studies alone at his home being out of contact with others, he will have superficial knowledge. ko(孤 gū)alone, isolated,orphaned,solitary,fatherless, ro(陋 lòu)hide,ugly,mean, vulgar,corrupt,plain, ka(寡 guǎ)few,tastless,scant,widowed, bun(聞 wén)hear,news,reputation,smell,famous,well-known,story, a surname.

248.  gu   mo   to   sho

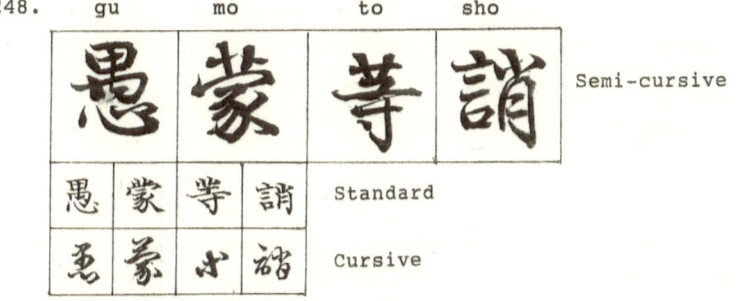

One will be a superficial person, and others also will slander him. gu(愚 yú)stupid,foolish,make a fool of, mo(蒙 méng)cover,receive, meet with,ignorant, to(等 děng)and so,ect.,and so forth,class, grade,wait,kind,sort, sho(誚 qiaò)blame,censure,scold,attack.

249.    i      go     jo     sha

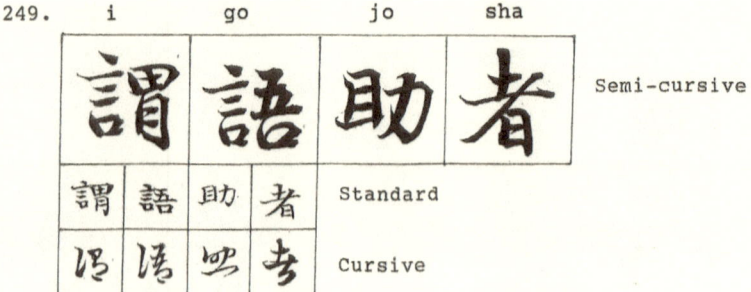
Semi-cursive
Standard
Cursive

Gojo(語助ǔ zhù) is words to help correcting a sentence by using particles, interjections.  i(謂 wèi)say,call,name,think, go(語 yǔ)language,words,tongue,say,speak, jo(助 zhù)help,assist,aid, sha(者 zhe)this,one,those who,thing,if.


250.   en     sai    ko     ya

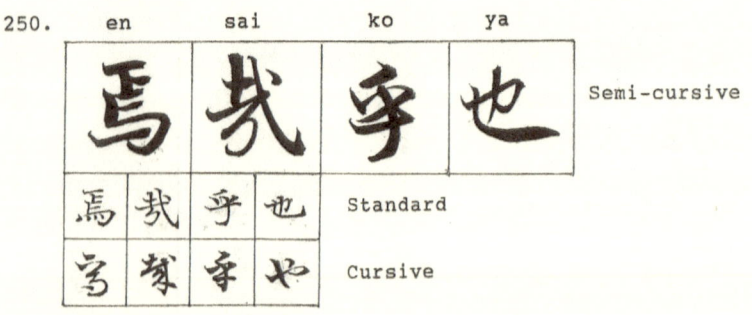
Semi-cursive
Standard
Cursive

Gojo is the following:   en(焉 yān)to,on,in,from,by,than, sai(哉 zāi)exclamation marker,used in exclamations, ko(乎 hū)Oh,question marker, ya(也 yě)also,is,too,well,still yet.

# 千字文

| 千字文 | 勅員外散騎侍郞周興嗣次韻 | | | | | | | | | | | | |
|---|---|---|---|---|---|---|---|---|---|---|---|---|---|
| | 天地玄黃 | 宇宙洪荒 | 日月盈昃 | 辰宿列張 | 寒來暑往 | 秋收冬藏 | 閏餘成歲 | 律呂調陽 | 雲騰致雨 | | | | |
| | 露結爲霜 | 金生麗水 | 玉出崑岡 | 劍號巨闕 | 珠稱夜光 | 果珍李柰 | 菜重芥薑 | 海鹹河淡 | 鱗潛羽翔 | | | | |
| | 龍師火帝 | 鳥官人皇 | 始制文字 | 乃服衣裳 | 推位讓國 | 有虞陶唐 | 弔民伐罪 | 周發殷湯 | 坐朝問道 | | | | |
| | 垂拱平章 | 愛育黎首 | 臣伏戎羌 | 遐邇壹體 | 率賓歸王 | 鳴鳳在樹 | 白駒食場 | 化被草木 | 賴及萬方 | | | | |
| | 蓋此身髮 | 四大五常 | 恭惟鞠養 | 豈敢毀傷 | 女慕貞潔 | 男效才良 | 知過必改 | 得能莫忘 | 罔談彼短 | | | | |
| | 靡恃己長 | 信使可覆 | 器欲難量 | 墨悲絲染 | 詩讚羔羊 | 景行維賢 | 克念作聖 | 德建名立 | 形端表正 | | | | |
| | 空谷傳聲 | 虛堂習聽 | 禍因惡積 | 福緣善慶 | 尺璧非寶 | 寸陰是競 | 資父事君 | 曰嚴與敬 | 孝當竭力 | | | | |
| | 忠則盡命 | 臨深履薄 | 夙興溫凊 | 似蘭斯馨 | 如松之盛 | 川流不息 | 淵澄取映 | 容止若思 | 言辭安定 | | | | |
| | 篤初誠美 | 愼終宜令 | 榮業所基 | 籍甚無竟 | 學優登仕 | 攝職從政 | 存以甘棠 | 去而益詠 | 樂殊貴賤 | | | | |
| | 禮別尊卑 | 上和下睦 | 夫唱婦隨 | 外受傅訓 | 入奉母儀 | 諸姑伯叔 | 猶子比兒 | 孔懷兄弟 | 同氣連枝 | | | | |
| | 交友投分 | 切磨箴規 | 仁慈隱惻 | 造次弗離 | 節義廉退 | 顚沛匪虧 | 性靜情逸 | 心動神疲 | 守眞志滿 | | | | |
| | 逐物意移 | 堅持雅操 | 好爵自縻 | 都邑華夏 | 東西二京 | 背邙面洛 | 浮渭據涇 | 宮殿盤鬱 | 樓觀飛驚 | | | | |
| | 圖寫禽獸 | 畫彩仙靈 | 丙舍傍啓 | 甲帳對楹 | 肆筵設席 | 鼓瑟吹笙 | 陞階納陛 | 弁轉疑星 | 右通廣內 | | | | |

# One thousand character poems (2)

都邑華夏　東西二京
背邙面洛　浮渭據涇
宮殿盤鬱　樓觀飛驚
圖寫禽獸　畫綵仙靈
丙舍傍啟　甲帳對楹
肆筵設席　鼓瑟吹笙
升階納陛　弁轉疑星
右通廣內　左達承明
既集墳典　亦聚群英
杜稿鍾隸　漆書壁經
府羅將相　路俠槐卿
戶封八縣　家給千兵
高冠陪輦　驅轂振纓
世祿侈富　車駕肥輕
策功茂實　勒碑刻銘
磻溪伊尹　佐時阿衡
奄宅曲阜　微旦孰營
桓公匡合　濟弱扶傾
綺回漢惠　說感武丁
俊乂密勿　多士寔寧
晉楚更霸　趙魏困橫
假途滅虢　踐土會盟
何遵約法　韓弊煩刑
起翦頗牧　用軍最精
宣威沙漠　馳譽丹青
九州禹跡　百郡秦并
嶽宗恒岱　禪主云亭
鴈門紫塞　雞田赤城
昆池碣石　鉅野洞庭
曠遠綿邈　巖岫杳冥
治本於農　務茲稼穡
俶載南畝　我藝黍稷
稅熟貢新　勸賞黜陟
孟軻敦素　史魚秉直
庶幾中庸　勞謙謹勅
聆音察理　鑑貌辨色
貽厥嘉猷　勉其祇植
省躬譏誡　寵增抗極
殆辱近恥　林皋幸即
兩疏見機　解組誰逼
索居閑處　沈默寂寥
求古尋論　散慮逍遙
欣奏累遣　慼謝歡招
渠荷的歷　園莽抽條
枇杷晚翠　梧桐早彫
陳根委翳　落葉飄颻
遊鵾獨運　凌摩絳霄
耽讀翫市　寓目囊箱
易輶攸畏　屬耳垣牆
具膳餐飯　適口充腸
飽飫烹宰　飢厭糟糠
親戚故舊　老少異粮
妾御績紡　侍巾帷房
紈扇圓潔　銀燭煒煌
晝眠夕寐　藍筍象床
弦歌酒讌　接杯舉觴
矯手頓足　悅豫且康
嫡後嗣續　祭祀蒸嘗
稽顙再拜　悚懼恐惶
牋牒簡要　顧答審詳
骸垢想浴　執熱願涼
驢騾犢特　駭躍超驤
誅斬賊盜　捕獲叛亡
布射遼丸　嵇琴阮嘯
恬筆倫紙　鈞巧任釣
釋紛利俗　並皆佳妙
毛施淑姿　工顰妍笑
年矢每催　曦暉朗曜
璇璣懸斡　晦魄環照
指薪修祜　永綏吉劭
矩步引領　俯仰廊廟
束帶矜莊　徘徊瞻眺
孤陋寡聞　愚蒙等誚
謂語助者　焉哉乎也

## About the Author

Hideo Muranaka received his BFA and MFA from the Tokyo National University of Fine Arts and Music in 1970,1972.

His pencil drawing was selected and he was invited to participate with The Pacific Coast States Collection from the Vice President's House at the Vice President's House, Washington, D.C.,1980 and exhibited at the National Museum of American Art, 1981. His drawing (pecil,ink) was awarded the Second Prize from the International Art Exhibition for MUSEO HOSIO in 1984 and First Prize, 1988, Italy. His calligraphy was awarded the First Prize from the Nogijinja ( general Nogi Shrine) Calligraphy Exhibition, called "Kensho" in 1961 and the numerous others.

Biographical data: Who's Who is American Art, 17th Edition; Men of Achievement, 1988, International Biographical Centre, Cambridge England, etc.

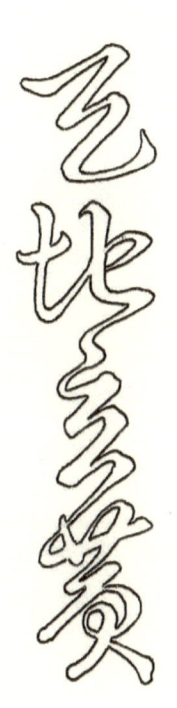

www.ingramcontent.com/pod-product-compliance
Lightning Source LLC
Chambersburg PA
CBHW031923240526
45464CB00022B/645